AF540588

Media Technology and English Language Teaching

Media Technology and English Language Teaching

Dr. Jameel Ahmad

A.P.H. PUBLISHING CORPORATION
4435-36/7, ANSARI ROAD, DARYA GANJ
NEW DELHI-110 002

Published by
S.B. Nangia
A.P.H. Publishing Corporation
4435–36/7, Ansari Road, Darya Ganj,
New Delhi-110002
Phone: 011–23274050
e-mail: aphbooks@gmail.com

2027

© Reserved

Typeset by
Ideal Publishing Solutions
C-90, J.D. Cambridge School,
West Vinod Nagar, Delhi-110092

Printed at
RD DIGITAL PRINTERS
Ansari road Daryaganj Delhi-110002

PREFACE

I had been feeling very strongly for a long time to find out some technological panacea for the problem of large classes and lack of motivation which are perhaps the biggest stumbling block to the successful teaching and learning of language skills. The exciting experience gathered from visual presentation instilled in me the yearning for the selection of a subject on the application of media technology to the teaching of English as a foreign language. An insight into the subject developed when practically I got used to listening to BBC broadcasting, BBC audio-video cassettes and many other standard BBC English programs on internet. This developed my conviction in the utility of media technology which was utterly neglected in developing countries in the past but now it is undertaken for sound empirical research. Contrary to this, in advanced countries, the scope of media technology has been fully realized and translated into successful practice. Hence Computer Assisted Language Learning (CALL) has now become an approach, in advanced countries, to language teaching and learning in which computer technology is used as an aid to the presentation, reinforcement and assessment of language learning on an interactive basis. Hence, interactive media resources are designed to engage students and to create an environment unique in fostering the integration of the four language skills (listening, speaking, reading and writing). Students become more autonomous and self directed in their learning. They are engaged with authentic language and authentic contexts. Teachers also adopt more learner centered methods in their language teaching. On the basis of ongoing development and evaluation, a variety of approaches and technical strategies have been considered to allow students to engage in real-time authentic language learning activities worldwide.

Since the emergence of the Communicative Approach, the need to meet authentic and meaningful EFL settings has increased.

Likewise, bringing to class artificially contextualized environment has decreased. In search for this authenticity, web-based learning has gained popularity and is exploited as a medium for student – centered, task –based and collaborative learning. The advent of the internet and new digital technologies are rapidly changing the role of the teacher and the nature of learning. The classroom teacher is no longer viewed as the repository of knowledge but as a facilitator who guides students to relevant digital information resources. Current generation teachers serve to assist students in organizing learning activities where students construct understanding around authentic and meaningful collaborative experiences. Thus web-based Computer Assisted Language Learning calls for a shifting role of traditional classroom hierarchy to a more balanced relationship between teachers and their students. Web-based CALL requires self-study (for autonomous learning), teacher-led instruction (for organization, monitoring, administering), and small group discussions (for interactivity). It allows learners to control selection, sequencing and the pace of learning, thus learners' accommodation of individual differences and use of learning strategies. These learning contexts and these teacher and student roles are met more effectively with the use of media technology. The learners and teachers have now realized that effective learning of English language will successfully take place if human resources, mechanical resources and teaching materials are made inextricably interwoven.

The basic aim of this book is to develop four basic language skills namely listening, speaking, reading and writing that the learners of English, in general, really need in pursuit of all their academic and professional careers. The major focus of this book is on how to learn and teach English effectively through the use of the internet, word processor, multimedia and hypermedia. It, hence, focuses on the promise of technology as a powerful tool for second language instruction and the challenge of training our teachers face in this instructional application. It explores how opportunities for the teaching of real English with real contexts are enhanced through media technology . It provides brief overview of how to implement technology enriched curriculum and how to make effective use of audio-video and computer assisted language learning programs in the class. Based on the fusion of theory and practice the book focuses the teaching of theoretical aspect of English sound systems and the learning of listening and speaking skills through numerous BBC English Language programs and websites available on internet.

The book discusses the integration of media technology into traditional instructional teaching methods to make learners acquire higher degree of proficiency and competence in listening, speaking, reading and writing skills. It contains synonyms, antonyms, idioms and phrases, usages and other vocabulary items. It incorporates guidelines for writing CV, sample of CV and the samples of different business letters.

The book is useful for the students, researchers and the teachers of all levels. This is also useful for both; the students learning English as a Second language (ESL) in common wealth countries, and the students learning English as a foreign Language.(EFL) in Middle East. It also emphasizes the teaching and learning of English sound systems so that the students can understand and learn the real English while listening to the native speakers on BBC cassettes and BBC websites available on internet. Short reading passages containing unique theme and contents and illustrating important vocabulary items and grammatical components have also been provided to improve the reading comprehension of the students.

I bow in reverence to the Almighty Allah whose benign benediction gave me the required zeal for the completion of this study. I wish to acknowledge the great debt I owe to the British Council Division of the British High Commission in India for its assistance in the form of books and video materials.

I would like to thank my esteemed teacher and guide Prof. F.U. Khan, professor of emeritus and ex-chairman, department of English, A.M.U.Aligarh, India. It was he who instilled in me thought provoking ideas about my career and ambition of life. I must place on record my heartfelt gratitude for his indigenous and brilliant suggestions.

For his immense encouragement I'm indebted to Dr. Abdur Rahim Kidwai, visiting professor of Leicester University, U.K. and full professor of English, department of English, A.M.U. Aligarh. India, a balanced and rare combination of modern and religious insight. His generosity and selfless support are praise worthy.

Part of this study owes its stimulus to my association with JCC, King Abdul Aziz University, Kingdom of Saudi Arabia. I finally planned to author this book in response to the students' immediate needs at JCC. The students pursuing different professional courses in the college need to acquire proficiency in general as well as in their specific fields of study. In this book, up-to-date methods and approaches with media technology have been recommended to improve students' integrated language skills. To all those, Dean , Vice Deans , HODs , my colleagues and the students of JCC,King Abdul Aziz University, Kingdom of Saudi Arabia I offer my sincere thanks.

I am immensely grateful to my younger brother, Dr. Sagheer Ahmad whose support deserves a special appreciation, and to all my friends in India and abroad. I am grateful to my father whose blessing remained a strong spiritual support throughout.

Immense thanks to Anjum Ara, a docile and innocent wife of mine beyond words, driving hassles away from me she always felt communion with me.

My kids: Sofia, Shehbaz, Asmar and Aiman who kept the house at storm thereby keeping it more alive, and revitalized, and me more sleepless to get glued to work. I feel immense love for them.

ABBREVIATION

ATS : American Telecommunication Satellite

CAI : Computer Assisted Instruction

CBI : Computer Based Instruction

CDI : Computer Directed Instruction

CALL : Computer Assisted Language Learning

CPU : Central Processing Unit

CCTV : Close Circuit Television

ETV : Educational Television

ESP : English for Specific Purposes

ITV : Independent Television

LTA : Language Teaching Association

NASA : National Association of Satellite in America

NALLD : National Association of Learning Laboratory Director

OCTV : Open Circuit Television

SITE : satellite Instruction Television Experiment

SDAIE : Specially Designed Academic Instruction Delivered in English

IPA : International Phonetic Alphabets

ASTP : Army Specialised Training Programes

CONTENTS

About the Author

Jameel Ahmad is an Assistant Professor of English at Jeddah Community College(a unique and paperless college),King Abdul Aziz University, Jeddah, Kingdom of Saudi Arabia, where he teaches integrated language skills: listening, speaking, reading and writing through electronic devices,

He obtained his Ph.D. in 'English for Science and Technology' (EST) from Aligarh Muslim University, Aligarh.India, and Post-Graduate Diploma in English Language Teaching from Central Institute of English and Foreign Languages (CIEFL) Hyderabad, India. Dr. Ahmad has also served as an editor of MAAS news letter. He has published various articles in reputed journals of ELT and ESP and translated twenty scientific articles from English into Urdu.

Dr.Ahmad has a unique identity as a successful teacher with more than ten years experience of teaching at under-graduate, graduate and post- graduate levels. He is one of the few EST teachers who has the passion for teaching Scientific English to the students of engineering and medical sciences. Dr. Ahmad has also worked at S.S School, Coaching and Guidance Centre and at the Department of English as a lecturer at A.M.U. Aligarh.India. He was assigned to teach ELT courses and English for competitive examination, such as teaching of essay writing for Indian Administrative Services, (I. A. S) English for Business Administration, and English for Railway Recruitment Examination etc.

Dr. Ahmad is presently working on a series of text such as

(1) English for Competitive Examination

(2) English for Businessmen

He can be contacted at drjameelahmad@rediffmail.com

About the Book

MEDIA TECHNOLOGY AND ENGLISH LANGUAGE TEACHING explores how opportunities for the teaching of real English are enhanced through electronic devices. It provides brief overview of how to implement technology enriched curriculum and how to make effective use of audio-video and computer assisted language learning programs in the class. Based on the fusion of theory and practice the book focuses the teaching of theoretical aspect of English sound systems and the learning of listening and speaking skills through numerous BBC English Language programs and websites available on internet.

The book discusses the integration of media technology into traditional instructional teaching methods to make learners acquire higher degree of proficiency and competence in listening, speaking, reading and writing skills. It contains synonyms, antonyms, idioms and phrases, usages and other vocabulary items. It incorporates guidelines for reading comprehension, writing CV, sample of CV and the samples of different business letters.

KEY FEATURES

(1) Focuses scope and salient features of Media technology

(2) Discusses the fusion of Media Technology into traditional instructional methods.

(3) It provides information about BBC audio video cassettes, BBC English Language Teaching and Learning websites and CALL Programs.

(4) Teaching of Phonetics and acquisition of Listening Skills,

(5) Learning of Received Pronunciation and speaking skill.

(6) How to write effective CV with the help of internet.

(7) Samples of CV and business letters.

(8) Different strategies to improve public speaking and to build up Vocabulary through internet.

(9) How to improve grammatical accuracy in written communication through internet.

(10) Learning of proverbs and saying through internet.

CHAPTER-1

FEATURES OF MEDIA TECHNOLOGY AND LISTENING SKILL

1.1.1 SCOPE OF MEDIA TECHNOLOGY

Over the past several decades, technology has become a fixture in many homes around the world. Its influence has permeated into all facets of life, including educational settings. This phenomenon has been hailed by many as the wave of the future in which language instruction will be driven by new advances in computer, the internet, high-tech gadgets and mobile technologies. Now the role of technology as a resource for English language teaching is increasing as educators recognize its ability to create both independent and collaborative learning environments in which students can acquire English with much ease.

Now the educators have realized that with the use of internet, word processor, multimedia, hypermedia and drill and practice programs, students can be engaged in individualized instruction designed to meet their specific needs and participate in cooperative projects that foster communication with peers in their classrooms and throughout the global community. This book focuses on the promise of technology as a powerful tool for second language instruction and the challenge of training our teachers in instructional applications. Multimedia computing, the internet and the World Wide Web have proved an incredible boost to computer assisted language learning (CALL) application. Once relegated to novelty status, CALL is finally achieving the recognition it deserves, thanks in large part to these developing technologies.

It is really noteworthy that the salient characteristic and benefits of a technology –enriched curriculum for English language learning underscores the pivotal role technology can play in English language teaching. **Krashen (1989)1** clearly suggested the need of comprehensible input in order for English language learning to take place. Perhaps the single most important role of English language teacher is to act as a facilitator in providing this intensive input. Traditionally teachers relied heavily on the use of pictures, and gestures to convey meaning to the beginners. The computer with its internet and hypermedia capabilities is a powerful addition to English language teaching resources. Computer utilizes a multi sensory collection of text, sound, pictures, video animation, and hypermedia to provide meaningful contexts to facilitate comprehension. Technology is equally important in the sheltered, academic- area classrooms where its ability to provide comprehensible input serves as a scaffold to support students as they study academically challenging subject matter.

The beginners of English language learning who are least exposed to English, in fact, lack motivation which can impede their language learning process. Because they remain passive through out. By acting as filters blocking comprehension **Krashen's** technology can assist teachers in creating a supportive and effective environment in the classroom. The interactive game features of computer programs and the exploratory quality of internet motivate students to use their second language. The untiring, non-judgmental nature of the computer makes it an ideal tool to help second language learners feel sufficiently secured to make and correct their own errors without embarrassment or anxiety.

1.1.2. ADVANTAGES OF MEDIA TECHNOLOGY

The students find enough opportunities with media technology to practice integrated language skills in the class. Because technology provides students with language experiences as they move through the various stages of language acquision. Students around the world can manipulate technology to solve linguistic problems and to learn language skills. They can utilize technology to support the writing process approach. Computer generated prompts, outlines, and other graphic organizers can be used for brainstorming and clustering. On-line databases offer students access to information on unlimited topics. Writing pen pals via electronic mail or chatting on the World Wide Web provides students with authentic audiences that serve as motivation for revising and editing their writing. Desktop publishing and hypermedia authoring programs give students a sense of pride of ownership and build self esteem as students publish attractive papers and reports. Authentic assessment is possible through a collection of student work in electronic portfolios. In addition to the samples of their work, students can import videos that explain their work and offer reflections on what they have learned.

Desktop computers are now able to play natural human speech together with full screen, interactive video, and an impossibility just a few years ago. Users can now communicate and interact with one another in real time. Such virtual chats provide solid opportunies for authentic language use among native and non-native speakers on an unprecedented scale in terms of the numbers of users and the geographical distances involved.

Though most drill and practice programs have the disadvantage of focusing on form over function, such software can be valuable in reinforcing class instruction and provide focused practice of specific skills. Pronunciation programs allow second language learners to visually compare the voice patterns of their speech with that of a native speaker. Drill and practice software can be programmed to adapt to the language proficiency level of each student, supplying corrective advice and self paced practice in grammar and vocabulary development. With individualized reading programs, students can select the difficulty level of the text as well as the speed of time readings. Today's individualized instruction utilizes multimedia to provide simultaneous practice of a skill areas- listening, speaking, reading and writing. Students can, for instance, read and listen to a story before writing and recording their own versions of a similar story. Programs with theme-based vocabulary embedded in context assist the learner in focusing on meaning before practicing form. Games provide additional motivation to individualized instruction by challenging students to move to the next level of mastery. Record keeping features assist the teacher and students in assessing the students' progress and designing future plans of study.

According to **Bickel**[2] The technology –enhanced curriculum employs multiple modalities to meet the needs of students with different learning styles and strategies. The aural, visual, tactile and kinesthetic learners have access to a variety of computer- based activities that are well suited to their preferred learning styles. As students perform diverse tasks with the computer, they broaden their repertoire of metacognitive , cognitive, and affective learning strategies.

1.1.3. Computer based technology, according to **Hunt**[3], has numerous advantages for second language instruction. It constitutes compelling arguments for comprehensive teacher training in the classroom use of technology. Research, however, suggests that colleges and universities continue to produce teachers who don't have adequate skills in utilizing computers for instructional purposes. Moreover, there is growing evidence that second language learners have less access to technology-enriched instruction than native English speakers.

The question then arises as to what contribution TESOL master's programs are making towards successful training of teachers in classroom application of technology for instruction of second language learners. **Butler's**[4] survey of 153 TESOL master's programs in the United States administrator responded to questions concerning the role of technology in their programs. The findings indicated that while TESOL master's programs had begun to integrate computer technology into their curricula, they had done so in limited numbers and scope. Forty two percent of the TESOL programs did not utilize any type of computer technology. Only 25% of the programs offered methods courses that provided teachers with skills needed to integrate computers into their second language learners used computers in their teaching, and sufficient training was cited as a primary reason for their failure to do so.

There were, however, some encouraging findings regarding course offerings. Fifty eight percent of the TESOL programs surveyed indicated some degree of progress in infusing technology into their programs. Eighteen percent offered a course specifically in computer assisted language learning (CALL), and over 35 % offered course that utilized computers for research purposes. In an investigation of the applications modeled in the TESOL curriculum, the three most frequently cited 'word processing, drill and practice software programs but also an understanding of the pedagogical issues involved in their use. Teachers need extensive training and practice with these applications in order to develop classroom lessons that capitalize on the strengths of the computer as a medium of instruction. The modeling of instructional uses of telecommunication networks reported by 26% of the respondents and multimedia by 21% suggested a growing recognition of the potential of these tools in second language teaching.

Over 21% of the TESOL programs reported providing instruction in the use of software that was appropriate for subject area instruction for second language learners. Many states now require pre-service and in-service training in delivering specially designed academic instruction delivered in English (SDAIE) Computers can clearly play a major role in allowing students to engage in academic tasks that focus more on their intellectual abilities than their language limitations. This survey revealed the limited progress yet promising potential of TESOL master's programs for teacher training in the effective use of technology in the classroom. Considering the multitude of benefits second language learners derive from a technology enriched curriculum, the task of adequately training their teachers in its application is a challenge that we dare not ignore.

1.1.4 The present study explores how opportunities for professional growth were enhanced through a process of electronically negotiated understanding as students shared topics of interest and posed comment on those topics. The idea of adopting technology for teaching purposes is appreciable. However, the process of implementing new technologies and managing radical changes is far from being a straightforward operation. The successful implementation of new technologies requires considerable effort especially by the administrative people involved.

It is argued that teachers should engage participants in the change process and that this increases the chance of successful implementation of innovation concerned. The underlying rationale is that a second language syllabus should reflect the systematic use of technology which facilitates the bringing of real acquisition e.g English language into the classroom.

Videodiscs have already made their mark in industrial training in the United Kingdom and are beginning to appear in schools and colleges. Whenever the learner is required to view something over and over again, the videodisc is undoubtedly an ideal medium. The videodisc player alone is a useful addition to the hardware used by the teacher in the classroom. Using the videodisc player and the hand-held keypad that accompanies it, the teacher can draw the attention of a group of the students to particular frames or sequences. Language teachers have a special interest in video as a medium, and are constantly searching for authentic video material, such as news broadcasts, documentaries and feature films. The main video medium currently available to language teachers is the videocassettes, which is used increasingly to make off-air recordings from satellite television broadcasts. So far as, however, language teachers have not been able to make much use of videodiscs. This is not due to lack of interest or willingness but, quite simply, a shortage of material. Whatever the advantages of videodiscs, the shortage of suitable recorded material explains why this exciting new medium is slow to gain acceptance by language teachers. The fact that it is not yet possible to record one's own material on a videodisc is probably the one major obstacle which overweighs all its other advantages.

Technology that encourages interactive learning can be an effective tool for teaching English language learners. Experts agree that ELT students are best served by technology that encourages interactive learning opportunities to practice communicating with real audiences. The use of technology in teaching second language has been increasing dramatically over the past few years. The universities in developed countries or in developing countries are implementing various technologies into the curriculum on a regular basis. This technology is becoming a bigger part of both in-class and home-study. As the traditional use of audio and film is supplemented by **Computer Assisted Instruction** (CAI) and interactive media technology. Computer by itself has many capabilities for enhancing language learning but combined with other technologies such as audio, video, modems and phone lines and satellites dishes, the possibilities are even greater for the second language learner. Information retrieval, many databases, many bibliographies and Multilanguage dictionaries are now accessible to students for research and language learning purposes.

1.2. TEACHER AND LEARNER WITH MEDIA TECHNOLOGY

There is a need to evaluate more profoundly the concept of educational technology to do away with the confusions which have created major obstacles in the considerable progress of learning English as a foreign language. **Alan Hancock**[5] explicitly defines the phrase, educational technology as follows:

Indeed the phrase educational technology has been coined principally to express the notion of men, machines and materials working together to improve the relevance of both teaching and learning process. Men, machines and materials are the three basic constituents which form the true concept of educational technology. Machines alone can't perform any significant role without equal involvements of men and materials, because all of them are equally important. The learners can not be fully benefited without the sincere cooperation of the teachers. In fact it is the teachers who deduce various devices to explain the aunthentic materials and to instill in learners the yearning for an efficient pattern of listening, speaking ,reading and writing. The misconception as regards the concept of educational technology can be eliminated only when it is considered not as a replacement for the teacher but as a complementary aid or as a tool to relieve teacher of tedious and repetitive tasks and thereby to concentrate to a greater degree on communicative aspects of language teaching. According to Alan Hancock, if men, machine, and materials are paid equal attention during the courses of teaching English as a foreign English, it'll make tremendous success.

By 'men' he refers to human resources which consists of the learner and the teacher. The most important resource the learners and his learning effort. His considerable response and his untiring efforts exercise a good deal of influence on language learning. Another human resource is the teacher who is the central and integral part in the learning system. However dazzling the success of modern invention, may be in the field of media technology, the teacher will always remain central as to help and guide the learner through interaction. The teacher imitates, organizes, arranges and presents the standard materials to the learners according to the needs of the students. It is he who checks the response, progress and the performance of the learners through input and feedback, so, it is essential for the teacher to build and maintain the motivation of the learners fostering dynamism in individuals and groups as the case may be.

With technology assisted instruction, there are changes in both educator and student roles. Students are given more responsibility for their own learning, while the educator serves as a guide and resource expert who circulates among students, working individually or in a small group with a technology assisted lesson. Educators observe more of the learning process in action and serves as a guide in that process. The new technologies offer many possibilities to the second language learner. The effectiveness of these technologies depends on appropriate use by informed educators. Neither textbooks nor technology can replace the live, unprogrammed feedback and interaction of the language teacher.

Teachers should use technology to help English language learners practice listening, speaking, reading and writing to support content based instruction and interactive activities with their peers who are learning. Drill and practice reading programs for all students designed by computer curriculum "**Corp**" and its components designed for English language learners called "**Discover English**" are invaluable for the students.

Inspite of numerous advantages the concept of introducing educational technology in language classrooms has been confined too narrowly. The common fallacy which has gone deep in preventing the teachers from the use of educational technology in the classrooms is the fear that it dehumanizes language learning and decentralizes the influences of the teachers on the students. More wrongly the use of educational technology in the classroom has been considered unscientific as it is supposed to be unanalysable. Such confusions arose in the mind of the people only when educational technology is considered as a separate entity which causes major obstacles in the way of English language learning and teaching. But the fact is that the role of the teacher is central even when the language is taught through educational technology because it is the teacher who must harness the power of media technologies in the classrooms and can choose to present media materials to the learners in the most suitable way in order to facilitate successful language learning and teaching.

1.2.1. THE ROLE OF A TEACHER

With regard to the use of video in the classroom , the role of a teacher is often misconceived . Those who are staunch believers in conventional pedagogic methods often consider video application as a substitute for the teacher, but the fact is that the teacher plays an eminent role in promoting active viewing and maximizing the instructional potentials of video materials. Hence the teacher still remains central in all teaching programs taken up with the aid of media technology as **Jack Lonergan**[6] states:

> *As in most language teaching situation the role of a teacher is key one. It is the teacher who must harness the power of video films; it is the teacher who has the prime responsibility for creating a successful learning environment.*

It is clear from the above quotation that video is undoubtedly a useful vehicle for language teacher to reinforce language teaching which does not mean to decentralize the role of the teacher, but it provides the teacher with authentic teaching materials and thus promotes the teaching of language skills. It enables the teacher to make tremendous contribution to developing language skills and facilitate successful motivation for the acquisition of target language by explaining video materials to the learners. Further it will be useful to argue that language teaching can be made more profitable if teacher is capable of creating interaction and communicative situations. In a CCTV workshop, it is the teacher who trains the learners as how to use video camera to bring maximum benefits to the learners. Just as the blackboards, flash cards are used in conventional method of English language teaching . Similarly video can be used in the classroom to promote learning of language skills. With some teachers it may be a new experience, because they are exposed to the video camera first time, but this initial difficulty could be overcome after a few days' training . **Jack Lonergan**[7] is quite right when he says:

> *It is usually inexperience, perhaps with a sense of awe of technology, Which leads teachers to these views. In fact the teacher's role is central because the teacher has to relate broadcast material to the language learner's needs.*

This is absolutely true that the success of language teaching through video depends almost on how dexterously the teacher has exploited the materials to the learners. Tremendous success in teaching language skills is most likely to take place on account of teacher's potentiality. Lack of teacher's serious involvement in video materials does minimize its cumulative effect on English language teaching. **Geddes** and **Sturtridge**[8] have given the following set of procedures for many types of aunthetic video material to be exploited by the teacher.

(1) The teacher should introduce video materials along with their linguistic features

(2) first play with sound to note key words and then ask one of the students to write key words on the board.

(3) Help students to reconstruct the strong line of the sequence from the key words / phrases.

(4) Second play followed by a general comprehension question.

(5) Third play preceded by discrete comprehension questions, missing words and sentences to be filled in during or after play.

(6) The teacher should hold feed back activities. e.g. discussion on the utility of the material and usefulness of the activities.

(7) So the question that video will decentralize teacher has no significance, because from the above discussion it has become quite obvious that the systematic involvement of the teacher in video application will yield successful results for learners.

1.2.2 THE ROLE OF LEARNER

The role of a learner is no less important than that of a teacher, because all the teaching devices will certainly go in vain if the learner fails to show his overwhelming interest or he exhibits his passive involvement, because passive involvement will lead him nowhere, so the learner should show his considerable response to video materials, which in fact, is a key to success in learning language skills. As the proverb goes, " the bigger the response, the higher the achievement". No successful learning of language is possible unless the learner himself carries on language learning process systematically and takes up the task of vocabulary building actively. Most of the students are viewing video only for the entertainment which can be a stumbling block in the way of language learning . So maximum seriousness should be induced in learners and passive viewing should be replaced by active viewing to promote interactive learning. What is essential for active learning is the fact that the learners should also be taught to record their own programs and listen to them carefully. In this way they will be able to pick up their own mistakes and only then they can take remedial measures to rectify them.

The performance of the learners should not be considered in isolation with video materials or the performance of the teacher, because all are equally important and complementary to each other. This has been well explained by **Lonergan**[9].

> *The role of the learner is to be a creative member in a joint partnership; the video equipment, the teacher and the learner.*

Cumulative effect of video application takes place only when a teacher, learner and video materials are equally taken into account. These three important ingredients play their distinct roles in language learning. If they are characterized by competence and authenticity, the speed of language learning will certainly be accelerated. He further classifies learners into two groups : those whose instruction is normally in the hands of the classroom teacher : and those who study at home by themselves . In both cases effective learning will take place only they are well motivated by video materials. By materials means standard materials which consists of structures, pronunciation, and the tone of standard model. The materials should also assimilate the cultural context out of which particular words emerged. Besides this, a corpus of linguistic pattern should also be presented on which the learner could model his own learning behavior in order to identify himself with social and contextual values of the country whose language he is learning.

There is no doubt that the fast growing demand for learning English across the world has given rise to a number of non-native varieties of English like Indian English, Filipino English, Nigerian English and so on. Though they have attracted good deal of attention, yet the learner should be made acquainted with the native model, because there is no dearth of such authentic materials. A number of agencies like BBC, Brighton Language Centre, Longman and Macmillan have come up with a very useful video materials for teaching English as a foreign language.

1.2.3. With the gradual acceptance of media technology its application has extended greatly to many areas of education specially into language learning and teaching. It offers many advantages to the teachers and to the learners as well. It is a powerful support to situational teaching because it presents authentic speech of the native speakers and the language is also introduced in the context of everyday situation. As a result of this the students learn by hearing and seeing the language in action. With regard to the scope of educational technology it will not be improper to quote **Sherrington**[10]

> *For the first time linguistic behaviour could be set in its total extraliguistic context; students could observe language as it really occurs, instead of experiencing it through a series of artificially created examples.*

Sherrington considers educational technology as an important tool for English language learning which gives learners the true picture of language as it is really used by native men and women in actual life, and it also makes them experience the proper use of language in the given context. In advanced countries, the scope of media technology has received a further impetus by introducing computer and internet in language classrooms which can be very effective means of instruction in foreign language learning if it is linked with a video disc recorder or a video cassettes player. The computer is used as an important tool for language learning. Its role in language learning is that of a medium far from threatening the teacher's position. Teacher's aim of teaching language skills is tremendously facilitated by computer.

Along with progress of science and technology, the methods and approaches of English language teaching also need to be modified to meet the challenge of the time. The rate of progress in learning language skills will be doubly enhanced if the students are exposed to technological innovations quickly. There is no doubt that learners' regular response to BBC audio-video cassettes will help them minimizing pronunciation errors and enable them to read dialogues flawlessly, because they contribute a lot to good habit formation through repetition of drills of native model. The errors can be identified easily and necessary correction can be made in order to make considerable progress in language learning. Apart from that, educational technology encourages active use of target language. It provides opportunities to build up fluency and promotes a sense of accuracy. It also offers opportunities to explore structure and grammar in ways appropriate to a wide range of language learners.

1.2.4. English language teaching primarily aims to develop four language skills namely listening, speaking, reading and writing. The goal of the teacher is to promote learners' competence in these areas. To obtain these goals has given rise rise to a number of methods and approaches.Most prominent among them are the grammar translation methods, the direct method, the audiolingual method and the communicative language teaching, which are still very common in government schools, colleges, and the universities of developing countries for teaching of English as foreign or as a second language, but in advanced countries they have been supported by media technology of which radio, tape, television, video cassettes and computer are the basic components. They have developed very fast in recent years and proved very useful for language learning by exposing learners to the stories and plays based on native models. More significantly the advancement of science and technology has made the students more technical minded and motivated them to learn English language through technological innovations. These technological innovations are frequently used in advanced countries, firstly because they have enough resources and secondly the people are more enthusiastic to keep pace with the fast developing technologies. On the contrary, in the developing countries the utility of educational technology is unanimously realized, but as yet it has not been used for English language teaching, first due to lack of resources, and secondly the awakening for educational advancement has developed rather lately. More particularly in India, the application of educational technology to English language is in fancy. Some open universities have initiated distance education programmes in the field of science, technology, medical sciences, management and journalism but they lack the resources in man and materials for the application of media technology to English language teaching. Television and video are used extensively in cities and villages for information and entertainment only. There are only a few instructional systems in country which could use media technology for teaching language skills. The teachers of English are still dependent on traditional methodology and hence the learners remain unexposed to educational technology. Besides the people are also found strictly adhered to traditional methods of English language teaching.

There is no doubt that educational technology has not been taken seriously in the mainstream of English language teaching, yet its advantages for the teaching of English as a foreign language are significantly realized. Educational technology is now considered to revolutionize and improve the whole methods and approaches of English language teaching, because it has immense potential to provide students with enough opportunities to gain access to natural and life like communication. The BBC audio-video cassettes are now available in abundance to provide the learners with clear native models.

In English medium schools, the students luckily, have enough chance to listen to the teachers who are quite efficient in language skills and capable of training their students in accordance with the native like model. But in Hindi medium schools the teachers are not well versed in English and the authentic materials are also lacking, hence the students are most likely to display very poor performance in learning language skills. In such schools and colleges, educational technology can play eminent role in English language teaching by using BBC audio-video cassettes in the class rooms. The teacher will be able to train first, themselves and their students too in native like pattern. These cassettes can also be used in English medium schools to quicken the progress and to make language learning much more authentic and worthwhile by way of enforcing certain fixed language skills. Now the people have begun to think that the use of modern technologies in the classrooms enables English language teaching to be much more meaningful, motivating and effective. It offers exciting possibilities of quicker access to authentic materials for rapid progress in learning language skills. It has potentials to stimulate the greatest number of senses. As, the learners who have been well exposed to radio., television, video and computer are most likely to acquire proficiency at a higher rate than their unexposed peers in terms of accurate acquision of listening, speaking ,reading and writing skills.

1.3.1. English Language Teaching Through Audio Equipments: Radio and tape-recorded are the two important audio equipments which increase the learner's potential to reinforce listening comprehension and to enhance his speaking skill as well.

A number of English programmes on radio transmission and the availability of BBC audio cassettes offer enthusiastic preparation to develop listening and speaking skills. It is anticipated that if learner responds to them carefully, he is most likely to learn listening and speaking skills at the higher rate. unfortunately radio and tape have not usually been recognized as an important vehicle for English language learning. The teachers and students have always remained oblivious of their utility in terms of learning language skills. As a result of this these audio equipments are still being used for no more than a source of entertainment. Their use has been further minimized by the availability of glamorous media such as video and computer which have attracted the learner a great deal owing to their visual presentation. However the enormous utility which audio and tape yield cannot be overlooked if they are properly used.

1.3.2. As regards the contrast between radio and tape it is quite worthwhile to mention that tape does offer enough convenience to the learner, because the learner is able to listen to it at any convenient time. On the other hand various programmes on radio transmission are also noteworthy such as programmes comprising drama, short stories and news put the learner in close contact with standard authentic materials. If the learner gets hooked to its careful listening since the inception of his learning period, his potential of listening and speaking will doubly increase, because the world of radio transmission opens new horizons which can be an important motivating factor, when applied to the teaching of English as a foreign language. One might say that it is a door which, when opened instantaneously puts one in communication with other people by way of English language which is used for international radio transmission. One needs only to turn on the receiver in order to pick up signals from all over Europe , England Scotland, Ireland, Germany, Poland, Greece, France, Italy etc. All the aforementioned countries use English as medium of communication in the world of short wave transmission. The learner's considerable response to the short wave transmission will certainly facilitate communicating in English by providing an excellent lesson of English language to learner and thus enabling him to feel confident in his ability to speak English in his day-to-day life. Besides, the learner is able to learn more about the people and the cultures of other countries.

1.3.3. With regard to the teaching of English through media technology it seems inevitable to mention that BBC English by radio is the first and foremost source of English language teaching, because it was first time during second world war that a number of programmes were transmitted for the teaching of English as a foreign language so that the people from all over the world could get acquainted with war news. Thus English language learning became a prerequisite to get detailed information about the ongoing war. The first English lesion by radio broadcast consisted of a series of selected utterances articulated slowly in perfect BBC English of the day followed by a careful translation in the language of learner. The basic purpose of this lesson was to disseminate war news across the world, which aroused enough interest among the people to attain rapid progress of English language with the end of world war 11 the interest of the listener increased consistently in the learning of English through BBC broadcast and thus more and more people got interested in the learning of English as a foreign language. As a result of this some more special bilingual courses at advanced level were devised in the fifties. The most popular and successful was the project to teach English to beginners entitled " Calling All Beginners" This was an excellent production of English teaching material which worked in a global context attracting large audiences from different parts of the world.

English by radio broadcast assumed still greater importance in 1960s when intermediate and advanced level courses in English were beamed not only to Europe but also to Asia. As television was confined only to the developed world, radio lessons in English were the only means available to the learners in distant developing countries. People in Europe in Middle East and Asia began to learn through another series of lessons "Walter and Connie" though it was basically a television series. Then occurred the refinement of radio vision which incorporated some of the advantages of visual support was known as radio vision or video vision in the context of open university. Radio vision was cheap, flexible and successful. It has been on the scene of media technology for a decade and its potential has been stressed enormously. Many teachers clearly find the contributions of radio and film strip most useful with the help of slide projectors.

1.4.1. RADIO: ITS LIMITATIOS AND SOLUTIONS

Inspite of all the advantages radio suffers from a number of inherent limitations. First it is a medium which depends on sound only and hence demands a habit of listening which is not ordinarily available to many. It is rather impossible to bring any well developed lesson in consonance with the convenience of the audience, because radio programmes can be heard only once. It may pass unheard if the learner isn't considerably attentive. Secondly no interference or control over the broadcast is possible to suit the special needs and interests of the learners, because it can't be turned on to be reheard at leisure. Moreover in radio programs there is no scope for interpersonal contacts. There is no interaction between the speaker and the listener. The listener can neither see the performance of the speaker, nor his facial expression, gestures and shrugs. On the other hand the speaker also can't see the listener , because radio transmission is entirely oral transmission with a complete absence of visual components. With a view to overcoming some of the limitations of the radio broadcasting, the following suggestions are given below:

(1) As the program is on the air, the listener can listen to anything only once, for all and every thing changes from moment to moment: so it requires listener's constant attention, because even his slight indifference towards the radio programme may cause the missing of valuable items. Hence it is necessary to have the radio program of amusing nature to sustain the listener's constant attention.

(2) Sound being the only medium in radio broadcast should be enriched by variety of amusing music which is most likely to captivate the listener's attention and sustain his utmost interest through out the program. This passionate listening may be considered as the only solution for the problems which radio broadcast faces. However it is unanimously considered that language skills can be easily accomplished by proper utilization of tape recorde

It seems indispensable to define first what listening actually means in broad perspective. Listening is the ability to identify and understand what others are saying. This involves the understanding of speaker's accent or pronunciation, his grammar or vocabulary and grasping the meaning of the speaker's speech.

1.4.2. The aforesaid components of listening cannot be fully obtained by radio, because radio cannot be stopped and played back. However in this regards, tape recorder has enough potentials in giving students excellent clear standard models to listen, relisten and to imitate. The teacher can also do the explaining by stopping tape recorder for a while and direct the students to mimic pronunciation, speech rhythm and intonation. Moreover when the teacher records his student's speech and plays back immediately, the students find it a highly motivating factor in listening to their own voices or the voices of their classmates. Students can easily trace out their own mistakes and thus will be able to improve the quality of their voice, pronunciation, accent, self evaluation and self expression. Hence the teaching of English language can be made more worthwhile if tape recorder is used in language classrooms and played back in order to relearn pronunciation, vocabulary, structures, intonation, words and phrases and so on . Moreover the task of language learning in the classrooms has been made easier by making BBC audio cassettes easily available to the learner. They are as follows:

1.5. BBC ENGLISH COURSES ON AUDIO CASSETTES

(i) BBC BEGGINERS , STAGE 1 (standard)

BBC BEGINNERS' COURSE is a forward looking course. Its syllabus, design and methodology are in line with the latest trends in language teaching. "**BBC Beginners" English course** satisfies all needs for learning a language by providing work on :

(a) Communicative skills e.g. English conversation etc.

(b) Fluency

(d) Correct pronunciation

d. Grammar and structure practice leading to writing practice.

This course deals with every day incidents such as meeting people, introduction, home. Planning journey, making arrangements, describing people, making comparison and so on. The course consists of a teacher's book a student's book and five cassettes

(ii) BBC Beginners, Stage Second (Standard)

This course is a continuation of stage 1 of **BBC beginners, English course.** Major features of this course are:

(a) Its presentation of the varieties of English as a language of internatic ıal Communication.

(b) Its coverage of the language required for simple but effective communication both social and professional context.

(c) It's learner centered and activity based approach.

After every few lessons, there is a lesson for checking what you have learned. By the time you complete the course you acquire a good command over English and use it with confidence in any situation at work or the social situations.

(iii) Keep Up Your English

This course is equally suitable for beginners and those who already have a good knowledge of English and wants to brush up. Basic grammar is dealt with completely. Translations of the first fourteen lessons is available in different languages.

(iv) Getting on in English (Intermediate English Course)

The course is suitable for those who already have an elementary knowledge of the English language. As the students of this level sometimes even make relatively elementary mistakes, simple revision points are introduced in the beginning of each lesson and are then developed to bring in more difficult structures. The textbook contains comprehensive language and grammar notes, exercises, and their answers and word lists beside the text of the recorded lessons. By the time the student completes the course he/ she will acquire a good command of the language, confidence to speak in different situations and sophisticated way of expressions.

(v) Choosing Your English (Advanced English Course)

This course aims to help the learner to widen his/ her range of expression by showing the style, idiom and intonation appropriate to various moods, situations and relationships. It concentrates not only on that is said but also on where and how it is said. For this reason idiom and pronunciation are given equal place with grammar and vocabulary. It will give the student a complete mastery over the English language. The textbook contains teaching notes, exercises, wordlist and drills. The drills are also recorded.

(vi) Make or Break

Make or Break contains 6 of the most dramatic stories in a series of programs specially made for the students of English.The programs use extracts from interviews with many of the main characters as well as contemporary BBC reports from around the world to build up the story. In the accompanying book, text of the recorded stories is given along with notes explaining some of the more difficult language used.

(vi.i) Buzz, Primary English Course

Buzz follows a carefully structure syllabus. It contains approximately 400 words and takes a complete beginner to a good elementary level . Buzz aims:

(a) to begin training children to think and to look for meaning using contexts, illustrations, words, sounds, numbers, colors and their existing knowledge.

(b) To focus on specific learning skills of memory, imagination and good study habits, it also encourages children to interact, cooperate and to work together.

(c) To get pupils used to communicating and interpreting body in spoken and written English.

(viii) Tiger's Eye

These audio cassettes provide across section of structures, tense, styles and registers. The context of the story allows the practice of many different language skills and functions, including taking messages, giving instruction, reporting telephoning, making appointments, asking questions and expressing opinions.

An important feature of both radio series and audio cassette recordings is the natural juxtaposition of India and British voices. It includes well known Indian actors with standard and regional accent . David Blake, as a native English provides natural model for British English . Tiger's Eye is thus very easy to understand for the beginners.

The availability of BBC audio cassettes makes English language learning appreciably faster. The BBC audio cassettes enable the students to achieve native like pronunciation along with greater degree of communicative competence. Hence the importance of tape recorder in comparison with radio is far greater. Moreover it offers some special advantages over the radio. As far as the adequate control of listening is concerned, the learner needs repeated practice which can be fully accomplished by tape recorder. Regular practice of learning authentic English by tape recorder provides the students with immediate feed back, by enabling them to master accurate pronunciation, intonation and accent. This develops enough confidence and provides more chance to practice and repractice the standard model.

1.6.1 Listening Skill: Listening is an integral part for learning any language, be it a foreign language, a second language or the learner's own language. It's illogical when the students sometimes say : I don't listen to the BBC news on the radio because it's too fast for me and I can't understand it . "that's a pity ! When it is too fast for you , when you can't understand it. That's exactly when !!! you need to listen to it. When you were a baby, did you understand your own language? When you were 3 weeks old, or 2 months or one year , did you understand everything ? Of course not! But you learned to understand by listening. Think about it you learned to speak your own language by listening to your parents, brothers and sisters everyday . After that you learned to speak . Then you learned to read . And then you learned to write . But listening came first.

First when a child hears the sound of his mother he feels loving and responds with smile. Mother's frequent sound serves as Skinner's "stimulus response theory" for the child to respond with smile. The child feels the import of what the mother tends to convey. Similarly a child cries when he feels hungry. On hearing it the mother quickly responds and feeds the child. So the child gets the import that he should cry whenever he feels hungry. Hence it could be deduced that the repeated stimulus and the repeated response will lead to the active process of learning. The child succeeds in learning words until two years. After two years he starts learning sentences. While listening to words and sentences repeatedly, the whole structure of the language also gets reinforced in his mind. In other words the child learns the language at lexical, semantic and syntactical levels unconsciously while listening to his parents. Here child's hearing is a biological process, so is his learning of language. In other words language learning is also innate. It is programmed in the child's mind.

Learners of English often have misconception about listening skill and hence confuse hearing with listening. As a matter of fact hearing is a biological function while listening is a function of intentional behavior. Listening is something we choose to do, and as such we need to build skills and practice to be effective at it. Teachers of English tend to teach English but in a haphazard manner. They don't know how to go about improving learners' listening skills and how to include some aspects of learners' attention thereby enabling them to improve listening skills tremendously.

1.6.2 Components of Effective Listening : There are two major components of effective listening need to be mastered. The first component is the teacher's ability to focus learners' attention on accent, intonation, words, body language and the actual meaning of the speaker. If teachers are unable to draw learners' attention on the aforesaid issues in a sustained manner. The learners will have difficulty understanding the nuisance of what the speaker is expressing. The learners have to be attentive while listening either to the native speaker or to the media technology. Because in terms of attention the learner of English can't be excellent listener.

(1) His attention drifts to other things running around his head while another person is speaking.

(2) He judges the speaker while he is speaking , thinking about how he could say it better. All these are going to imped the learner's task of understanding the speaker from the speaker's viewpoint.

(3) The listener spends most conventional time eagerly waiting for his turn to speak

(4) The learner rehears his response while the other person is speaking

(5) The learner undertakes some other activity while the other person is speaking (e.g. checking the time, making extensive notes, answering the phone etc.

In other words, since listening doesn't come naturally so the learner is required to sustain his attention and discipline in order to acquire this skill with most appropriacy and propriety. So all that is required is television or radio and a few minutes of uninterrupted time available on a regular basis. The learner should listen uninterrupted to a sermon, speech, lecture or telecast of parliament or government proceedings.

The listener should also record news bulletin from the radio and television and listen to them over and over until he gets the gist of what is being said. Each time he listens, he will understand more and more. So he should listen enough times until he is able to write a short summary of what is going on .The most important thing is to let the radio or cassette or television or record play. Your brain will hear , your subconscious will listen and you will learn. Once the learner gets used to listening habits , he starts listening repeatedly. Consequently he is most likely to develop the ability to focus his attention on speaker without being distracted by judgments and thoughts that he generates internally. However if the listener doesn't learn how to focus his attention he is least likely to understand the speaker. As the learner improves this ability he will find himself much involved in the act of listening thereby understanding the message in its totality. By recording the show or just using one of the shows' recordings available on the websites he'll get a chance to listen to the same edition of one show more than once.

With regard to listening skills there are four principal venues that are frequently used in order to develop listening comprehension skills in English as a foreign language (EFL) learners. By integrating these resources, the EFL teaching professional can effectively aid learners not only in listening comprehension skills development but also in multiple aspects connected speech production. Understanding a listening passage can be made all the more difficult by four key influential factors. By four key influence factors, including the number of speakers in the passage, the technical difficulty, the level of spoken material in the passage, the speed of the speech and the accent of the speakers in the passage, and whether or not there is any external support provided for the listening passage.e.g. photos, illustration, graphics, vocabulary review or pre-listening activities.

If the EFL teacher is a native or non-native English speaker, then dialogue can be modeled in addition to modeling pronunciation and connected speech examples. If the EFL or ESL teacher isn't a native or near native speaker and this teacher doesn't have sufficient speech and pronunciation in English to model these aspects for the learners then other English speech modeling and input sources can be used, Besides, we must not limit learners by thinking they can only learn and improve in particular way. A valuable audio visual aspect is to provide to English as a foreign (EFL) learners by native speakers. Produced CDs and DVDs. Speech and cultural elements can be illustrated or documented using authentic audio- video materials such as movie clips and documentaries students produced and TV programs or audio cassettes or CD- ROM.

A wide range of CDs and DVDs exist to provide native speech modeling of different speaking pronunciation, national and regional English accent, multiple varieties of English are commonly used through out the world and having examples of these by which learners can be exposed to the differences in spoken English will be helpful. In demonstrating pronunciation variables. Online over- the-air and cable radio broadcasts can be especially effective and are reading available in much of the world.

Three examples of excellent online radio broadcasts sites are:

(1) *www.live365.com*

(2) *www. Archive.org*

(3) *http://www.* Multilingualbooks.com/online-radio.html

ONLINE AUDIO

Increasingly, institutes of higher learning are making integrated online materials available to learners. These may consist of spoken dialogues, video dialogues, short stories, interactive games, connected speech examples, movie clips, interviews, documentaries and even pronunciation lists. Learners can log into the website at their institution to receive extended practice and materials to complement in class learning. Many large well established universities. Institutes and ELT materials publishers are making such materials available online to both clients and the general public. In addition, specialized websites for English language teaching have cropped up in abundance and offer a plethora of materials and didactic assistance for the ELT professional.

Some examples of available materials online include:

(1) Penguin-*www.penguinenglish.com*

(2) Pearson-Longman *www.Longman.com*

(3) Heinemann-http*://www.heinemann.com/*

(4) Oxford University Press www. oup.com

(5) Cambridge University Press- *www.cup.org*

(6) Heinle and heinle-http*://www.heinle.com/esl-d/*

(7) McGraw-Hill-educational resources *http://mcgraw-hill.co.uk/kingscourt/*

(8) Harvard University-open courseware.

(9) *http://oedb.org/library/features/236-open* courseware - collection.

A web search using "Online English Language Teaching materials" will yield a virtual bonanza of materials: planning and resources for the time –strapped English teacher. English teachers should be resourceful in identifying and acquiring materials to augment their classes in proving as broad a variety of listening comprehension materials as possible for their classes. Thus by integrating any all available resources, any English language teaching professional can effectively aid learners not only in developing their listening comprehension skills but also in the demonstration of multiple aspects of connected speech in worldwide Englishes.

1.6.3 Phonetics and Listening Skills

Knowledge of theoretical aspect of phonetics will facilitate the learners to understand the native speakers of English. If the learner is able to understand the accent and intonation patterns of English sound he can easily understand the native speakers of English. It 'll be difficult for the learners 'who are learning English as a second language or as a foreign language, to understand which sound is produced with high pitch sound and which one with low pitch sound. It will be immensely useful to integrate theoretical aspect of phonetics with media technology in which native speakers of English could be seen and heard.

Phonetics

It is the study of sound of any given language. It has three aspects: **(1)Articulatory Phonetics:** It describes how vowels and consonants are articulated in various parts of the mouth and throat. **(2) Acoustic Phonetics:** It describes how sounds are transmitted from the speaker's mouth to listener's ear. **(3) Auditory Phonetics**: It studies how the speech sounds are perceived and decoded by the listeners.

Phone: The actual sound produced, such as simple vowels or consonant sound. E.g./p//b/,/k/,/g/./i/,/i://e/etc.

Phonology : It deals with the way speech sounds behave in particular languages or in languages generally. Hence it marks the way languages use differences between sounds in order to convey differences of meaning between words. Phonology describes that spoken language can be broken down into a string of sound units.

Phonemes: A phoneme is the smallest "distinctive unit of sound" of a language.It distinguishes one word from another in a given language. This means changing a phoneme in a word produces another word that has a different meaning . In the pairs of words "**cat** and **bat**" the distinguishing sound **c** and **b** are both phonemes.

Allophones: A phoneme may have several allophones, related sounds that are distinct but do not change the meaning of a word when they are interchanged. For example / t / in "tea" and / t / in "trip" are allophones of the phoneme / t / .

Accent : The degree of prominence a syllable has. It varies from with cultures, regions, regions and speakers, but there are two major standard varieties in English pronunciation: British English and American English. Within British and American English there are also a variety of accents. Some of them such as Received Pronunciation (RP) and General American (GA) received more attention from phoneticians and phonologists.

Received Pronunciation: It is defined as "educated spoken English of **Southeastern England**". RP is close to BBC English(the kind of English spoken by British newscaster and presented in most British dictionaries). It is a social accent associated upper classes or people who have attended public schools in Britain. They follow **non-rhotic** accent, hence they pronounce **"r"** only if it is followed by a vowel- right , rain, room , Robert, far away. On the contrary the speakers of General American (GA) follow Rhotic accent and pronounce "r" in all positions.

There are 26 alphabet letters in English but there are 44 speech sounds. To represent these basic sounds the linguists use a set of phonetic symbols called the "International Phonetic Alphabet(IPA) . The chart below contains all IPA symbols used to represent the sounds of the English language.

Vowel Phonemes			Consonant Phonemes		
01	/ɪ/	pit	21	/p/	*pit*
02	/e/	pet	22	/b/	bit
03	/æ/	pat	23	/t/	time
04	/ɒ/	pot	24	/d/	door
05	/ʌ/	luck	25	/k/	cat
06	/ʊ/	good	26	/g/	get
07	/ə/	ago	27	/f/	fan
08	/i:/	meat	28	/v/	van
09	/ɑ:/	car	29	/θ/	think
10	/ɔ:/	door	30	/ð/	that
11	/ɜ:/	girl	31	/s/	send

12	/u:/	too	32	/z/	zip
13	/eɪ/	day	33	/m/	man
14	/ɑɪ/	sky	34	/n/	nice
15	/ɔɪ/	boy	35	/ŋ/	ring
16	/ɪə/	beer	36	/l/	leg
17	/eə/	bear	37	/r/	rat
18	/ʊə/	tour	38	/w/	wet
19	/əʊ/	go	39	/h/	hat
20	/aʊ/	cow	40	/j/	yet
			41	/ʃ/	shop
			42	/ʒ/	leisure
			43	/tʃ/	chop
			44	/dʒ/	

(1) The vowel (A) may have the following pronunciations·

1. (a:) far (fa:)
2. (æ) fat (fæt)
3. (∂) ago (∂g∂u)
4. (ei) date (deit)

(2) The vowel (E) may have the following pronunciations:

1. (e) ten (ten)
2. (∂) teacher (ti: tʃ ∂)
3. (3:) herd (h3:d)
4. (i) become (bicΛm)
5. (i:) even (i:vn)
6. Silent "e" taste (teist)

(3) The vowel (I) may have the following pronunciations:

1. (i): pity (p I t i)
2. (i:) kilo
3. (ai) write (ra:it)
4. (∂) family (f æ m ∂ l i)
5. (3:) dirty (d3:t i)

(4) The vowel (O) may have the following pronunciations:

1. (:) organ (: g ∂ n)
2. (σ) got (g σ t
3. (Λ) color (k Λ l ∂)
4. (∂) doctor (d σ k t ∂)
5. (∂ u) October (σ kt ∂u b∂)
6. (u) do (d υ)
7. (u:) move (mu:v)
8. (∂) more (m ∂)

(5) The vowel (U) may have the following pronunciations:

1. (u) put (put)
2. (u:) rude (ru:d)
3. (∂) culture (k ltʃ ∂)
4. (3) purse (p3:s)
5. (Λ) up (Λp)
6. (u ∂) sure (ʃu ∂)

(6) (Y) as vowel, (not as a consonant), may have the following sounds:

1. (i) pity (piti)
2. (ai) July (azu:lai

Integration of theory and Practice in the teaching of phonetics will be of immens help for the students. If students learn the theoretical aspects of these phonetic sound system they will quickly undertand the accent, intonation and the overall pitch variation of the speech used by native speakers of English. It is hence recommended that the teachers of english must know these symbols and they should also teach them to the students.

REFERENCES

(1) Krashen, Stephen. (1989). Language Acquisition and Language Education. New York: Prentice Hall International.

(2) Bickel, B and Truscello, D. (1996) TESOL Technology : New Opportunities for Learning : Styles and Strategies with Computers . TESOL Journal , pp. 15-19

(3) Hunt, N., & Disdier ,A (1994) Teaching future teachers to enhance teaching and learning with technology. Technology and Teacher Education Annual. (1993) (pp. 178-182)

(4) Butler- Pascoe, Mary Ellen, (1995). A National Survey of the Integration of Technology into TESOL Master's Programs. Technology and Teacher Education Annual, pp.98-101

(5) Hancock, Allan. (1997) Planning for Educational Mass Media, London 5

(6) Lonergan ,J. (1984) Video in Language Teaching . p 25

(7) Lonergan, J. (1983) Video Application in English Language in ELT documents Oxford, P. 74

(8) Geddes and Sturtridge. (1982) Ed. Video in the Language Classroom in the Use of Video Films.by David Kerridge London P, 113

(9) Lonergan,J. (1983) Video in Language Teaching, London , P.24

(10) Sherrington, Richard, (1973) Television and Language Skills, London, P. 12

CHAPTER-2

Integration of Media Technology into Traditional Instructional Methods

2.1.1. AUDIO VIDEO AIDS IN ENGLISH LANGUAGE TEACHING

Sound and vision are the two important modalities which constitute the basic components of audio visual aids. The association of words and phrases with visual pictures enriches vividness and offer thorough elucidation of the whole context. The importance of audio visual aids is further confirmed with the realization of communication as the main goal in learning of English language. Thus the communicative language teaching gave rise to the direct method of language teaching which can be fully achieved by audio visual aids. The visual picture on the screen brings forth the complete communicative situation, and promotes creative power by sparking of learners' sensuousness and sensitiveness. Moreover the integration of sound and vision lays profound effect on the learner by depicting real life situation, real life people and real life language. Not only does the learner learn to decode and understand the verbal elements of target language but he also learns to incorporate aural clues such as intonation and pauses, paralinguistic information such as facial expression, gestures, register, social setting and cultural behavior. So by making use of these audio visual elements in a class, the passive learner can be turned into active learner. By tickling his interest and providing him access to television and video supplements. English language teaching can be done more effectively. It provides enough exposure to the wide variety of cultural context. This is unanimously accepted that the understanding of culture does lead to the understanding of the language. There is no doubt that television and video not only entertain the audience but they also bring an air of reality into classroom and provide students with authentic speech forms of standard models.

2.1.2. The latest development in teaching methologies centers around communicative approach in which the comprehension of meaning, contextualization and pronunciation are of paramount importance. Almost all the eminent features of communicative approach find their best exposure in audio visual aids through which English language teaching gets consummated. In television and video, paralinguistic features and visualization enormously promote English language teaching. One finds speaker on the screen conveying meaning to his dialogue partner through arm movements, facial expression gestures, context and so on. Moreover the speaker and the other participants in the dialogue can be seen and heard. The language learner can easily see the age, sex, relation, dress, status and the feeling of the participants. Similarly the setting of the communication becomes more clear because the language can be seen on the screen where the action is taking place. These information may further help to clarify whether the situation is very formal or perhaps informal. All these components present complete communicative situation and develop considerably the learner's fluency and his communicative competence.

2.1.3. Television provides learners with adequate control of listening skill and enables them to recognize the range of segmental and super segmental features of English through visual presentation of speech that promotes understanding where the learners are incapable to understand. This is, in fact, true that every listener requires to recognize the particular phoneme in English sound system, for example, the problem of teaching an initial s/ th distinction, sink/ think. Sank/ thank, sick/ thick, which can be handled fairly well by television . Full understanding of these words which have almost similar pronunciation can be fully achieved if they are associated with visual picture on the television screen.. Moreover television can make speech practice more meaningful by producing pictures in visual mode while giving the auditory information in the sound mode. Keeping this in view much emphasis may be laid on the use of television for the teaching of English, because during the course of listening to the speaker on television we watch his lips movement and observe some of his important gestures which help our understanding of the utterances. A classroom teacher who endeavors to demonstrate the position of the tongue for the English / i / in lips, or the lip position for the vowel sounds in " Lock" " look" or " took/ talk" will find difficulty on demonstrating them satisfactorily for the benefit of the whole class. Television can show the movements of the articulatory organs with great precision either by close-ups of speaker's mouth or by filmed or diagrammatical representation of what happens to the organs of speech in particular articulation.

2.2.1. Advantages of Television Television is an audio visual medium which has enormous potential in sustaining the viewer's interest to the point where the participation becomes so active that he starts responding carefully to the ongoing information and vocabulary . Both, the concerned information and vocabulary are indispensable to achieve competence in language skills. Hence the learners are hereby advised to watch television not for entertainment only but for achieving proficiency in language skills. Now if anyone claims that television isn't accessible to the masses is rather unjustifiable, because television has reached almost every house and it can be used by the parents to enhance the children's vocabulary of English language. Besides this, the relevant informations the learner gathers from TV programs on any subject develop in learner enough confidence and this also facilitates communication, because the things which promote communication most are the relevant informations and the working knowledge of the language. Both are equally important. This is, in fact , true that one can't speak if one doesn't know what to speak. Similarly if one doesn't know the working knowledge of English, one can't communicate himself properly. So it will be quite proper to say that both are supplementing each other in developing communicative skill of the learner.

2.2.2. Teachers and learners of a foreign language are confronted with the problem of provision or restoration of context. We learn our own language in its context. Here again " Close Circuit Television" (CCTV) will prove its worth. We gradually associate words with objects and behavior, because the people who speak the target language use the words in relation to their behaviors and those objects. Classroom teaching of foreign has often been absolved from the context but the television has the popular strength that it deals with what are Obviously real life and here now stimulations. The Situations are presented to the students and dealt with by the teacher and to their manifest reality is added the Tremendous value of complete visibility.

Mac Lean[1] that television offers enough stimulation to the learner and the visual clues manifest real life situation and real life language and thus promote the learner's understanding of the language. Language skills are usually recognized as listening, speaking, reading and writing. Listening skill concerns the recognition of sound and quick understanding of the meaning of the whole sentence. Speaking skill involves complete communication along with correct pronunciation, accent and the rhythm of the language. Reading skill involves the recognition of written words. The writing skill involves the correct representation of the ideas in written form. Speech and writing originate in the speaker/ writer, who wish to communicate. This requires the speaker or the writer's imagination for correct and appropriate use of words in accordance with the context. The listener/ reader needs to decipher the connotative and denotative meaning of the script , and listener how to understand the spoken words and phrase and the whole contextual meaning.

We now turn to the possible uses of television in order to examine the kind of contributions which television might make to the development of listening and speaking skills.

2.2.3. Video has proved to be the most useful resource for English language teaching, because no other technological aids play as important a role as video. Apart from its being the combination of sound and vision, video offers the facilities of freeze frame, rewind and re-play. Video recorders can be used to store programs for showing at any convenient time. On the contrary, television broadcast is ephemeral and usually one way. If the viewing time has not been used well by the learner, he will not be able to avail himself of the opportunity. Likewise video recorder, tape recorder too presents similar facilities, but due to lack of visualization, it fails to create equal effect on the learner. A number of advantages of video are also found in radio, tape recorder and television, but they don't offer the same facilities for the use of classroom material and content that video recorder does. Some other features of video recorder which are also shared by other related media are the presentation of real life situation and complete communication. In this regard Jack **Lonergan**[2] firmly states:

> *Video brings a slice or real life into the classroom. It presents the complete communicative situation, Language learner not only hear the dialogue, they also see the participants in the surrounding where the communication takes place. The visual information not only leads to a fuller comprehension of the spoken language but can also benefit learners in a number of other ways.*

From the foregoing quotation, it becomes quite clear that learner is able to see the behavior and social relationship of the participants and can also perceived how people react when they are angry, sad, sarcastic, thought, impolite and so on. Expressing his views on the effectiveness of video, **Wills**[3] also writes

> *That is precisely because of the moving visual component That video is popular aid in the language classroom, at least With teachers trained in its use.*

Wills believes that the visual component of video is one of the major factors in promoting the learners, understanding of the language in its totality. Visual pictures completely remove the vagueness and the complexity of the conversation and thus supplement the learners' understanding. Thus video cassettes can prove to be quite significant for complete understanding of the language. The types of video programs which should be prepared for English language teaching are as follows:

1. Video recordings of language teaching broadcasts and films.

2. Video recordings of domestic television broadcasts, such as comedy programs and news programs.

3. Video recordings of specialist films and television programs, such as documentaries produced by industry or educational programs.

4. Video language teaching materials made for the classroom rather than for public transmission as broadcasts.

5. Self made video films involving the teachers and the learners.

These self made video materials should have specific learning goals relating to developing new vocabulary, variety of language structure and communicative ability. The thing which is worth mentioning in this context is that video materials should be authentic so that the learners can be exposed to the authentic language of the native speakers which is a bit difficult to understand in the beginning. But learner can overcome this problem by listening to the variety of authentic materials regularly.

A variety of video materials along with brief introduction are as follows:

FOLLOW ME PART I

(I) Follow Me Part II

" **FOLLOW ME**" provides essential skills for everyday communication. It can easily be adopted to suit a wide range of learning context. Light entertainment, drama and documentary methods of presentation are all employed and entertaining. Comedy sketches are used to illustrate important teaching points. Step by step it takes absolute beginners to a level at which they can communicate with confidence in English on every day matters.

(II) On We Go

" **On We Go** " is a video series with supporting materials for new beginners. The first twelve units revise a number of documentary structures and establish a basic vocabulary. The video dialogue is spoken clearly and slowly, with frequent pauses.

(III) Person to Person (intermediate)

" **Person to Person**" is a course with supporting materials designed to enable students to understand and use a repertoire of expressions that relate to several essential language functions and to handle these expressions appropriately on the specific context in which they are being used.

(III) Bid For Power

Bid for Power" is "a course of English for the advanced learner. It is aimed at people who need to develop English language skills for negotiating with other speakers and representing their firms in English speaking environments through out the world. The video component for " Bid for Power" is in the form of a drama serial set in the world of international commerce and industry. The cultural settings and business practices are international rather than specifically British or American or the special activities in which business people are involved, are given prominent attention.

(V) Teaching Observed (For Teachers)

It enables teachers to watch other teachers at work and to adopt what they see to suit their own circumstances and the needs of their own students. It is designed for use in teacher training institution.

The theme of the " teaching observed" is that the language taught in the classroom must prepare students for the language of real life., whether at work or in other subjects that they will study in English. A single lesson can't show how a class develops practical language skill. A single lesson can't show how a class develops practical language skills. So " Teaching Observed" also shows the development of supplementary reading and reference skills and the ability to write letters, reports and essays.

(VI) Video in the English Class

It illustrates ten activities to help teachers make more productive use of video. There are silent viewing, freeze frame, role-play, behaviors study, prediction, thinking and feeling, sound only, watcher and listeners, telling the story, culture comparison. It further offers guidelines which can be adopted to suit the needs of the individual teacher. Each strategy has been developed to encourage a lively communicative atmosphere in the classroom.

(VII) Muzzy in Gondoland

This is a lively new beginners' course for children. An action packed animated cartoon acts as a powerful and stimulating language teaching tool while at the same time entertaining young learners with a story about Muzzy, friendly monster from outer space and his friends. To make sure that children understand the language in the video, a character called Norman appears time time to time and explains important teaching points in a simple but effective way.

(VIII) BBC Business English

"**BBC BISINESS English**" is a study pack for business people who want to use English confidently at work. The business dialogue and documents are supported by a range activities and study aids. It contains lively dialogues , which illustrate how business people talk on telephone, in meetings, at conference, and on social occasions. It also contains letters, memos, reports and other documents to provide , reading practice and model for writing. These exercises designed to develop vocabulary practice , grammar and promote speaking and writing tasks.

(IX) English Pronunciation

It has been designed to acquire correct pronunciation by describing systematically the characteristic sound of spoken English and its stress, rhythm and intonation. Some more special courses for business English are:

(a) The language of business

(b) Business communication

(c) The Financial English

(d) Export English Course for Business Executives

(e) Take a Break

(f) Medically Speaking

(g) Key to Business English

2.3. VIEWING ACTIVITIES

In order to exploit aforesaid video materials fully in the classroom, one should integrate the following activities in the lesson

PREVIEWIN

anticipate

VIEWING

Present

EXPLOTATION

Compare

Practice

Communicate

POST VIEWING

Reinforce

FOLLOW UP

Consolidate

These activities depend on the selected material student-needs; their ages and instructional objectives. A teacher may choose to integrate all these activities in a given lesson. The activities presented below are, for the most standard communicative activities that have been adopted for use with films and video materials.

2.3.1. Previewing Activity

The primary purpose of previewing activities is to prepare students for the actual viewing of a film/ video materials. Hence the teacher should give the class a task before hand to make the students listen with more attention at the time of actual viewing, so that language skills could be enormously improved . A few suggestions in this regard are as follows:

(1) The class should listen to a typescript of the video sequence and imagine what is happening . Where and when , why and what type of people are involved.

(2) The class should be divided into a number of small groups, so that every individual learner can be engaged in discussion and every viewer can be enabled to come out with his own comments and remarks.

(3) Textual information of the topic should be handed out to be read and discussed before hand to elicit or extend existing knowledge. On the basis of this information the class can discuss how the topic can be visualized and what location can be used.

(4) The transcribed dialogue of the video sequence is read aloud by the learner for pronunciation, intonation and stress . After the film clip is shown , they can discuss the differences and practice certain aspects.

(5) Students should examine the title of the film/ video in order to hypothesize its content. This quick activity can be done in a class or in small groups.

(6) In order to involve learner in brain storming activities, the teacher can pose questions or elicit information that link student's past experiences with the video material . For instance if the film STUNTMAN accompanies a unit on " Profession" the teacher can involve the students in the following activities. The teacher should incourage the students to think of such five professions that can be dangerous or have risk. The students then

should be asked to write down the risks of those professions and interview the students from other groups by such questions –would you like to be—— why? Why not?

2.3.2. Effective Viewing Activities

There is no doubt that sound and vision are the two important components of video which are normally played together, but sound and vision can be played separately in order to lay specific impact on the learner. Thus in order to encourage language activities , the video can be presented to the class in four ways:

(1) Viewing Straight Through

(2) Sound On Vision Off

(3) Sound Off Vision On

(4) Viewing in Parts

(1) Viewing Straight Through

When a video sequence is shown right through, it presents the learners for what they are about to learn and familiarizes then with the whole context . Showing straight through, the students should be prevented from the task of note taking and completing worksheets, otherwise they are most likely to miss some of the important visual information. The basic aim of showing straight through is to give learner the glimpse of video material as a whole, so the video cassettes should be shown without interruption

(2) Sound on , Vision off

It means to remove temporarily the visual element of video tape and listen to the program without visual presentation . Such practice can be used to mark a notable contrast between presence and absence of vision and ultimately enable the learner to conclude that he will be missing a lot of things due to continuous absence of visual presentation. But the thing which is worth mentioning is that the vision is removed temporarily to reinforce, listening comprehension which can be fully achieved if the learner's attention is, for a while, kept detached from vision.

(3) Sound off And Vision On

Removing the sound from a video presentation leaves the learners with only visual components and persuades him to understand and anticipates the meaning with the help of visual clues. Such practice puts the learner's imagination at work and then promotes his ability to understand paralinguistic features such as arm movement, facial gestures and eye contacts.

One more thing which reveals the utility of such practice is that if video is stopped or made slow moving, the visual clues can add comprehension of more than just words and can prove to be more meaningful as the indicator of mood, emotions, or temperament of the speaker which are the psychological aspects of communication are integral parts of language learning. Apart from this, the learner can be asked to interpret what these visual clues actually mean. Afterwards, the sequence is shown again with sound and differences are discussed. Such practice can also be used to enhance writing skill. The learners can be asked to write what they have perceived through visual clues. Thus visual elements can be exploited to make the learner's imagination fertile and prolific.

(4) Viewing in Parts

The video material can be divided into various parts and shown for a number of times so that audio and visual elements of each parts can be fully understood. In this regard Margaret Allan is quite right when he states that controlled presentation is indispensable for effective learning, so that more attention could be laid on visual clues, paralinguistic features, contextual information, video sequence and so on.

Viewing in section deals primarily with breaking up a programme into various sections. Any program can be broken up into section and the learner can be guided through one section at a time. Within a long program, it is easy to find a short sequence which contains exactly what the teacher wants for a particular lesson. Such control over video text gives teacher the flexibility to use it the way that best suit particular purpose at any particular time.

Viewing in sections comprises the following techniques which are shown below in stages.

(i) Set previewing questions for section one.

(ii) Play section one with picture and sound with pauses if necessary.

(iii) Discuss answers for section one questions set previewing questions for section two

(iv) Play section two with pauses if necessary.

(v) Discuss answers for section two questions.

Set previewing questions for section three , then the whole programme without pauses can be repeated. Different sections can be treated in different ways for teaching listening comprehension, grammatical structures or writing skills. The teacher should also show the frozen pictures to the learners with pauses in order to teach paralinguistic features. A variety of techniques can be used to make the program effective and interesting. If a program is done in sections, the teacher should try to finish all the sections and finally play the whole program through. This technique of the final extended viewing all make significant contribution to the comprehension work.

Under this method the video materials are viewed more intensively to use language for its vocabulary, structures, pronunciation and intonation and thereby to focus attention on register and non-verbal features. It also promotes the practice of communication among learners to develop a general awareness of this visual medium. Some suggestions for the effectiveness of this technique are:

(i) The learners work in pairs. Learner A watches a small segment of the video ,though without sound, while B listens to the soundtrack only or reads the transcript of that segment. B describes the setting and the kind of people involved without giving away the actual text. A will listen and afterwards fill in the missing information or make correction. This little task will enhance careful listening to each other and stimulate communication.

(ii) The class is given a number of scrambled sentences describing certain scenes or scrambled lines of the dialogue they saw. The students are asked to rearrange them and put them into right order order after they have viewed the video film.

(iii) The class is given worksheets containing several questions (open, right/ wrong, multiple –choice) or a grid to be filled in, matching statements, or other kinds of language activities.

(iv) The class is given a gapped version of the spoken text. When they fill it in, before viewing , it specially aims at textual comprehension and reading strategies . Filled in after viewing , it intensifies the listening.

(v) A section of the video clip is shown , but the teacher stops it for a few times to ask the class to predict the next sentence aiming at intensive listening for punctuations, structures and context. Now at the stage of second viewing the class watches the video merely to reinforce what they have learnt in terms of vocabulary, structures, functions or general understanding of the language in relation to subject matter. Finally comes the stage of FOLLOW-UP which means to develop further the learner's communicative competence and to stimulate response and activity. Some possibilities at this stage are as follows:

(1) Roleplays

(2) Interviewing each other

(3) Class debates

(4) Class makes its own commercial.

(5) News bulletin

For the learners at early stages, the role of video is mainly to expose them to realistic samples of language in a real life situation, in which there is much visual support to facilitate global understanding . At this stage practice should be simple. Controlled and repetitive . With learners at an intermediate level it is essential to expose them to more complex and less controlled situations in order to make video rather a stimulus to elicit response or a medium to focus more on language in relation to the topic.

With learners of advanced levels, video is mainly a stepping stone into the area of fluency and free communication. Video integrated into learner's lesson or syllabus, will most certainly provide him with a unique and enjoyable learning experience , provided the material is used constructively with a variety of learner centered activities. The teachers should be fully aware of the medium , being another useful aid, not meant to replace him/ her but merely to support them in their teaching. They can give maximum benefits to the learners if they are really competent in handling video equipment.

2.4 INTEGRATION OF MEDIA TECHNOLOGY IN ENGLISH LANGUAGE TEACHING METHODOLOGY

When teaching methodology is coordinated with educational technology in English language classroom it doubly enhances the effectiveness of teaching in terms of interest , motivation ,accuracy and competence of language skills. The integration of media technology into traditional teaching methodology has marked tremendous success in advanced countries, because the situation for using media technology in advanced countries is fairly ideal due to advanced level of educational system . In developing countries the use of media technology for the teaching of language skills remains still a contentious issue. Because the people believe that the use of media technology distracts teacher from his direct contact with students. So they don't intend to the integration of media technology within the framework of language teaching skills. In fact the developing countries require English most urgently as part of their development programmes yet in these countries English is still taught through grammar translation methods . Besides this, the teachers are neither efficient nor well trained. As a result of this the goal of learning/ teaching English as a second language is not properly achieved. There is no doubt that media technology was beyond reach in developing countries due to lack of adequate resources but now the students have access to all the necessary educational tools. It'll yield a tremendous success if it is tactfully used in the classroom . Educational technology presents the chunks of authentic language within the whole context and enable the students to experience it in a controlled environment. Radio, television , tape recorder and computer are powerful means to motivate students for learning English with interest. Therefore this unit is mainly concerned with the application of these modern technology to prove how they can lead to effective learning environment.

2.4.1 Integration of Media Technology into Direct and Audio-lingual Method

The main emphasis in Direct Method of Learning is on learning of target language by keeping direct relation of foreign words and phrases with objects without the use of mother tongue. Its basic aim is to develop the ability to think in the target language. On the other hand , the basic tenet of audiolingual method lies in hearing and repeating of model dialogue individually and then in chorus. It lays emphasis on pronunciation, intonation and fluency. The learners are encouraged to memorize dialogue line by line without recourse to grammar and mother tongue. Both methods refrain learners from the use of mother tongue and advocate that meaning should be conveyed through demonstration and action. The supporters of theses methods expect that the fluency of the students will increase enormously during the course of their conversation.

In Direct Method the teacher has to associate acts and objects with certain combination of sounds in order to reproduce the foreign words or phrases or to have a clear idea of the objects described orally by the teacher. If visual elements are supplied through television and video the achievements and the success of the methods will tremendously increase. It'll also save time energy of the time who verbally tries to associate the foreign words with objects of the experience of learners Besides, the technique in Direct and Audio lingual Method focus upon the pronunciation, intonation and the speech. What else could give a better understanding of phonetic interpretation and paralinguistic features than television and video. The phonological level of listening skill is fully understood by the learner through television and video which operate through two modalities , sound and vision.

In Direct Method of language teaching the use of mother tongue in the classroom is discarded but sometimes it becomes quiet difficult to perceive the form of some objects for those who are learning English as a second language, if they are not supported by their mother tongue. Therefore complete comprehension of the objects unknown to learners will take place only when their visual pictures are provided. Hence in case of using video the teaching will be increasingly facilitated in terms of accuracy , pronunciation, intonation and more significantly the full understanding of the objects. Let us consider how the visible context supports or modifies our production or comprehension of verbal message. While speaking, we assume a body of shared knowledge is derived from a common visual context. It is impossible to assign any value at all to the words **what's it like** ? if they are taken out of it. Likewise the words ***It's cold*** may refer to the weather , the tea or the water or any other number of possible Things. Through visual elements, all these information or statements can be contextualized and complexities can thus be minimized. Paralinguistic features particularly the movements of head and hands are commonly used to indicate the importance attached to a particular utterance .

2.4.2 Integration of Media Technology with traditional methods of teaching

This evaluates as to how educational technology successfully enters the domain of traditional methology of teaching English as a foreign language, and how it can be integrated as a powerful aid to achieving the objectives of each method. More significantly, it will be useful to mention how far the different elements of educational technology discussed at length in previous chapters could go a long way in achieving the goals of teaching English as a foreign language. But it will not be out of place if the basic aims of prevailing traditional methods are precisely discussed. The methods which will particularly be taken into account are direct method, audiolingual method and communicative methods of language teaching . If they are effectively supported by media technology, they will add delightful experience to learners and thus the basic aims of English language teaching will be remarkably achieved.

Direct Method of language teaching is diametrically opposed to the use of mother tongue for the teaching of English as a foreign language. It advocates that the meaning should be directly conveyed through demonstration and actions, and the language should be taught by using it actively in the classroom and every thing should be done in target language without the use of explicit grammar. It becomes now clear that direct methods of language teaching places heavy emphasis on interaction between the learner and the teacher in target language and promotes the use of target language in communicative situations usually without recourse to the native language. According to the Modern Language Association in 1901, the direct method of language teaching has been described as follows:

> *In its extreme form the method consisted of a series of monologues by the teacher interspersed with exchanges of question and answer between the instructor and the pupil all in the foreign language …… . A great deal of pantomime accompanied the talk . With the aid of this gesticulation by attentive listening and by dint of much repetition the learner came to associate certain acts and objects with certain combination of the sounds and finally reached point of reproducing the foreign words or phrases. Not until a considerable familiarity with the spoken word Was attained was the scholar allowed to see the*

foreign language in print. The study of grammar was reserved for still a later period. **Cole, R**[4]

The quotation explicitly reveals that the basic aim of Direct Method of Language teaching is to enable the learner to understand the speaker of target language and learn how to communicate his ideas adequately in that language. In direct method of language teaching , mime, gestures and contexts are used to elicit questions and answers without the use of mother tongue.

In addition to this, intensive oral interaction should be held in target language and learner should be taught to develop direct association between forms and meaning. It can be stated more precisely that direct method of language teaching persuades the students to practice the following principles and procedures.

(1) Classroom instruction should be conducted exclusively in the target language.

(2) Oral communication skills should be built up in a carefully graded progression organized around question and answers exchanges between teachers and students in small intensive classes.

(3) Grammar should be taught inductively. Concrete vocabulary should be taught through demonstration, objects and picture: abstract vocabulary should be taught by association of ideas.

(4) Correct pronunciation and grammar should be emphasized:

The principles are seen in the following guidelines for teaching oral language, which are still followed in contemporary Berlet schools:

(1) Never translate: demonstrate.

(2) Never explain: act

(3) Never make a speech: ask questions

(4) Never imitate mistakes: correct

(5) Never speak too much : make students speak much.

(6) Never speak too loudly : speak naturally.

(7) The various oral psychological or phonetic methods developed at beginning of 20th century have been grouped together by **Wilga Rivers**[5] as forms of direct method; in that they advocate learning by direct relation of foreign words and phrases with objects and actions, without the use of native language. The ultimate aim was to develop the ability to think in the target language.

The audiolingual method was in its embryonic form in the 11 world war in U.S.A . There was an increasing need of such army personnel who were proficient in the speaking of foreign languages. The methodology for the fast training of army men in foreign language was derived from intensity of contact with the target language rather than from any well developed methodological basis. This program was known as Army Specialized Training Programme (ASTP) . It didn't have any underlying theory . However, it did convince a number of prominent linguists of the value of intensive, oral based approach to the learning of foreign language. Moreover, a growing demand for expertise, in teaching of English as a result of the coming of thousands of foreign students to join American universities (for these students had to be well versed in English before some specialized course) , led to the emergence of the American approach to ESL, which by the mid-50's had become audiolingualism.

Audiolingual approach was a combination of structural linguistic theory, contrastive analysis, aural-oral procedures and behaviorist psychology .Behaviorism like structural linguistics is scientific in its approach. To the behaviorists the human being learns by modification of behavior and is capable wide repertoire of behaviors. The occurrence of these behaviors is dependent upon three things: a stimulus, which elicits behavior. (2) a response which is triggered by a stimulus : and (3) reinforcement, it serves to mark the response (behavior) as being appropriate or not and encourages the repetition or suppression of the response in the future since audiolingualism is primarily an oral approach to language teaching, the process of teaching involves intensive oral instruction. The focus of teaching is on accurate speech. There is almost no provision for grammatical explanation or talking about the language. As for as possible, the target language is used as the medium of instruction . translation or use of native language is discouraged.

In a typical audiolingual lesson the following procedures will be observed:

(1) Students first hear a model dialogue (either read by the teacher or on tape) containing the key structure. They repeat each line of the dialogue, individually and in chorus. The teacher pays attention to pronunciation, intonation and fluency. The dialogue is memorized gradually, line by line. if necessary a line may be broken down into several phrases. The dialogue is read aloud in chorus.

(2) Certain key structures from the dialogue are selected and used as the basis for patterns drills of different kinds. These are first practiced in chorus and then individually. Some grammatical explanation may be offered by the teacher at this time, but this is kept to an absolute minimum.

(3) The students may refer to their textbook and follow up reading ,writing or vocabulary activities based on dialogue may be introduced . At the beginning level writing is purely imitative and consists of little more than copying out sentences that have been practiced. As proficiency increases, the students may write out variations of structural items they have practiced or write short composition on certain topics. Audiolingual methods can briefly be interpreted as speech based instruction with primary objective oral proficiency and

it dismissed the study of grammar or literature as the goal of ESL.

The audiolingual method aims at teaching the language skills in order of listening –speaking, reading and writing. The emphasis is in the ealy years is on the language as it is spoken in every day situation. Moving at advanced levels to the more literary forms of expressions Rivers Wilga thinks that the Audio Lingual method in spite of its immense popularity among the foreign language teachers , has not been free from serious criticism by theoretical linguistics. Wilga Rivers herself has judiciously assessed the strength and weaknesses of the audio lingual method in the book "Teaching Foreign Language Skills". Wilga Rivers thinks that the teaching materials are more scientifically and systematically designed, reading and writing are not neglected. Learner's motivation in audiolingual classes is on the whole high. Students enjoy learning to use a language from the very first day of their introduction. The techniques advocate active participation by all students for most of the time. But at the same time the author points out the pitfalls in the methods . Students trained by audiolingual methodin a mechanical way can progress like well trained parrots. They are uncertain of what they are saying and unable to use the memorized material in real life contexts. Challenging audiolingual method of learning **Noam Chomsky**[6] (1958) argues that language acquisition can not take place through habit formation because there is far too complicated to be learned in such manner.

Communicative Language Teaching

The shortcoming of audiolingual method gave rise to the communicative approach in language teaching which starts from the theory of language as communication. Its basic aim is to enhance the student's communicative skills outside the classroom. The communicative approach to language teaching was strongly supported by **Widdowson and Brumfit**[7]. They felt the need to focus in language teaching on communicative proficiency. For communicative competence grammar is not a prerequisite. Because any grammar based methodwhich supports to communicative skill will fail with the majority of the students. Only a few will be able to improve communicative competence through a grammar course.

The central principle of several prevailing modern method is to acquire communicative competence to use the language for real communication for which exercises and drills cramming emphasized in the Direct and Audiolingual method. Are neither sufficient nor necessary. **Newmark and Reibal**[8] stated this principle.

> *Systematic organization of the grammatical form of The language material exposed to the learner is neither Necessary nor sufficient for his mastery of the language. Presentation of particular instances of language in context Which exemplify their meaning and use is both sufficient and necessary.*

Communicative activities engage learner in communication and require the use of such communicative process as information sharing, negotiation of meaning and interaction. Communicative activities can be divided into two categories (1) Functional Communicative Activities. (2) Social interaction activities. Through functional activities the learner is placed in a situation where he must perform a task by communicating as best as he can. The success can be measured by the facts that how effectively the task is performed. In social interaction activities on the other hand the learner is placed in a situation where he is encouraged to consider the social context. This produces speech which is appropriately suited to the specific situations.

Language is a potent means to approach one's innerself, because it is through language one conveys his views and imparts his happiness. / sorrow to others. It mediates between writer/ speaker and reader/ listener by giving full understanding of what is latent in their minds. On the other hand it enables learner to apprise himself of scholarly contributions of some renowned personalities . so learning language without full understanding of the meaning is almost futile.

Comprehension Method

Keeping in view, the recent advances, **Herris winitz**[9] lays much emphasis on the importance of comprehension in language acquisition . He is of the opinion:

> *That comprehension should be the focal Methodology in the acquisition of a foreign language. Students and teachers by mistake often insist that instruction in speaking and grammatical principles should play the fundamental role in learning to master a new language. The teaching of understanding or comprehension seem to be of secondary significance.*

This quotation reveals that the basic aim of language learning is to comprehend the meaning first and only then the instruction of speaking and grammatical principles should be given to the learners . Comprehension training doesn't mean to put restrain on speaking in the classroom . Though the focus of attention is mainly on the understanding of the meaning yet speaking is not discouraged.

According to **Balasco**[10], speaking is not only allowed but encouraged. However the central objective of the language exercises is the comprehension of meaning . Those who advocate the theory comprehension in language learning believe that comprehension is an active and dynamic instructional system. In order to lay much emphasis on comprehension methodology Balasco further points out the shortcomings of the audiolingual method saying that this method provides student with a corpus of memorized sentences but there is no guarantee that meaningful production will follow. He comically noted that : students are capable of manipulating Drills and memorizing dialogue to a very high degree of proficiency, yet despite the case in which they perform in this area, not many students can understand and speak the language outside the ordinary classroom situation.

Audiolingual method undoubtedly makes learner able to manipulate language, yet it doesn't lead learner to any successful communication outside the class because of its having least stimulating factors for comprehension. So far as the successful communication is concerned comprehension training is a highly successful approach. The application of comprehension approach for language learning can be easily examined by some of the significant investigations. One of the investigations deals with the adults who had significantly poorer aptitude in foreign language as measured by Modern Language Aptitude Test. With only thirty two hours of comprehension training, they were compared college students who completed either one or two college semesters of German. The adults on account of their increased comprehension potentials were markedly superior to college students in listening skill. Another investigation deals with the application of comprehension approach to teaching Spanish to college students for three hours, one evening a week devoting a total of ninety hours of instruction . the average performance of students in listening , reading , writing and speaking was equivalent to that of college students who had 200 hours of instruction. Often when other people hear about the application of comprehension method for the teaching of foreign language, they equate it with the conventional method which means speaking in the classroom at the cost of grammatical exercises. But the fact is that both differ greatly with each other . Comprehension training as a methodological approach doesn't provide the learner with a set of explicit rules. But its goal is to bring in contact with a wide range of language data systematically presented so as to facilitate the process of understanding and then the explicit understanding of the grammar will automatically develop. Since the communicative and comprehension approaches are meaning based in contextual situation , they can be strongly supported by educational technology. Because they promote understanding by visual presentation which demonstrates better view of behaviors, social situation and everyday language of native speakers. Media technology contributes a lot towards the challenge of new emphasis on developing communicative competence and promoting sharp comprehension potential in the students.

2.4.3 Integration of Media Technology in Communicative and comprehension Approach

The teaching of language as a system of communication implies that teaching will be focussed to a great extent, on a view of languages as to be used fluently outside the class. For the communication to be successful, mutual interaction and full comprehension of the subjects are indispensable, because they provide the students with great incentive which successfully facilitate communication . Comprehension approach develops enough confidence and persuades the learners to do away the hesitation. It has been explicitly proved that comprehension of the subject matter can be tremendously achieved by visual elements. So far as mutual interaction is concerned video can present successful interaction and more significantly can show why misunderstanding occurs and how to avoid breakdown in communication.

There can be a more powerful support in following and assisting the communicative theory in language teaching which aims to provide learners with a fluent command of a linguistic system for communicative purpose in the first stage. The structural facts can be better learnt with a video. Recognition of structures in speech is made easier when the learners see and hear them in different situations. For example a heard structure " **he has been pushed into water**" could also be depicted with picture illustrating someone. This structure-picture relationship shown on the video is a good example of presentation or practice work.

In the second stage of communicative theory, the total skill of communication in different types of communicative situations is practiced. The learner is put in a situation where he must perform a task by communicating functional as well as social interaction activities. Both activities are interrelated and the teacher may begin a teaching unit with a communicative activity such as role play. The context for language introduction is best provided by the teacher through the video showing a real life situation .

The most important advancement in language teaching efficiency was language laboratory in the fifties which was considered to be powerful aid for teaching language skills. But its utility has been outdated by more recent invention of television and video, because television and video have enough potential to promote almost all the basic language skills where as language laboratory is confined to the skills of listening and speaking only. Moreover the laboratory work becomes boring and repetitive and reduces the learner's keen interest. The audiolingual exercises were once being practiced when language laboratory was much in use.

But they can be more effectively practiced now by television and video . From the point of view of cost, space and utility, the use of mini- lab relatively seems to be more feasible proportion. Mini lab has almost the same function which a language lab has except that it doesn't have the console and individual learner uses it according to his need . It is less expensive and instead of having ten and twenty booths in language lab we would have a few mini labs at a much lesser cost. There are enough resources for English language learning on internet. They could be fully utilized if language labs are available. The following sites could be used for teaching purposes.

2.5 AMERICAN ENGLISH WEBSITES FOR ENGLISH LANGUAGE LEARNING

CNN News 24-Hour Non- Stop headlines, World News, US News and weather news.

Voice of America (VOA). The VOA newsroom has live news via the internet as well as a seven day archive. If you want to listen with a radio, schedules and frequencies can be found here.

America's Public Broadcast Service Online Newshour

There is a text only version of this which you can use to check your listening comprehension.

Interactive Listening Comprehension Practice

Produced by Doug Mills from the Lingua Centre at the University of Illinois. This site has a number of interactive listening comprehension exercises based on excerpts from American radio and TV programmes. These exercises are best for intermediate to quite advanced learners. Try it!

The English Listening Lounge

Learn English by listening. Study any time, any place . It's easy and it's fun. Listen to real people speaking real English . your English'll improve quickly.

Foreign Language for Travellers. Basic words and expressions in a wide range of languages , both text and sounds . You can also search for a particular word / phrase to be translated into all the languages.

The Yamada Language Center: records a wide variety of programming every weekend. The weekend schedule broaden the cultural scope. This allows language students a chance to peer deeper inside the country they're studying and foreign students to get a taste of home.

English Pronunciation: Guide to Pronunciation: This page gives the pronunciation symbols from the Merriam –Webster Online Dictionary

The International Phonetic Alphabet; This is the full pronunciation chart produced by the International Phonetic Association.

English – vocabulary & Grammar: CNN Newsroom for ESL. An excellent site to practice English grammar and vocabulary with authentic news articles based upon a weekly CNN broadcast throughout the school year.

Other Sources of English

CBC Radio on the internet: This is the Canadian broadcasting Corporation's radio station. The site uses real audio so you can listen live!

World Radio Networks (WRN) WRN broadcasts international news and feature programming from public radio stations in over 20 countries around the world via satellite, cable and the internet.

Radio Australia's Asia Pacific Programme is broadcast live on Saturdays. *Audio Archives* at date back to April 1998. There is a useful link to Regional Extra which has a list of articles related to the archived radio programmes.

RTHK on line : live broadcasts of radio programmes in English. The files can be either sent as a continuous stream to your

PC or you can download them and listen to them in your own time and at your own pace.

Time cast: The Real Audio Guide. A complete listing of Real Audio Broadcasts from around the globe concerts, video , radio and TV . Take a look!

English- References your Dictionary.com : More than 150 dictionaries. Multilingual dictionaries, thesauri and other vocabulary aids, language identifiers and Guessers, and index of Dictionary indices and a web of on-line grammars.

Merriam – Webster On Line: provides a free, searchable on line dictionary and thesaurus, word games, a word of the day and many other English language and vocabulary reference tools and resources.

Multilingual Tools and Services. Links to online dictionaries, search engines, and other resources, in a variety of languages. materials are categorized according to grammar items and dates. Don't miss it.

Word Watch : Weekly commentary on a common word or phrase taken out of the Bank of English – **COBUILD's** database of current English. The commentary not only offers a definition of the word or a phrase but also discusses interesting details about its usage.

Longman Dictionaries: This site has word games, study exercises and lesson plans.

World Wide Words: Usage Notes, Short articles about words that often cause problems.

LEARNING

First Sight , second thoughts: looks at the lives of six people who have settled in Britain. Read and listen to their stories and then try the exercises 4 video and 2 audio narratives.

The Learning group: Personalized learning Games . create your own language learning game online (as a java applet) or play games created by other authors.

Interactive Learning Resources: vocabulary and comprehension exercises based on CNN New stories. You can read as well as listen to the new stories.

Grammar Safari, the Lingua Centre: This site includes lots of suggested activities to learn about how particular grammar items are used in www materials . Particularly good for independent learners or teachers.

Online Writing Labs: Online writing Room the mission of the Writing Room is to provide an open teaching and learning environment for the collaborative discussion of writing so that students may become more aware and independent writers.

TC's Online Writing Lab Help with essays, research papers, writing tutors , helpful documents.

Paradigm Online Writing Assistant : writing informal essays , thesis, argumentative essays , exploratory essays, and documenting your sources.

Quotations : Quotations Collections including Advice (good and bad0 proverbs, Annoying proverbs, wit, famous leaders, recent, wisdom, Miscellaneous Malapropism, posters with quotes.

The Quotations Page : a large site devoted to quotations from famous people and literature. Over 10, 000 quotations are available for searching and browsing . includes the popular quotes of the day .

Dictionary .com: free online English dictionary , thesaurus and reference guide , crossword puzzles and other word games , online translator and word of the day.

Encyclopedia .com: more than 14,000 articles from the Concise Columbia Electronic Encyclopedia , Third edition has been assembled to provide free quick and useful information on almost any topic.

Encarta ® Online Home Encarta : online is the home for the Encarta Concise encyclopedia , the Encarta schoolhouse educational site and Encarta Explore, an ever –changing resource for exploration.

Encyclopedia Encyber Pedia. The Living Encyclopedia. Good Sections on Common errors in English, Online English Grammar, and Writing resources online.

Films provide complete visual images along with aesthetic pleasure which sustain learner's interest by arousing his maximum senses. Films can be the main vehicle for English language learning . Through them, contextual background can be made real, because they bring real picture of culture, behavior and temperament of non native speaker into the classroom and thus make viable atmosphere for English language learning. In movies speech is associated directly with action which helps in removing L1 inference of mental translation. But the problems which can be generally associated with movies is that the students can be possessed by their entertaining elements, so, the teacher should use them dexterously in the classroom by undertaking a number of oral and written activities. Some suggestions, in this regard, for the teachers as well as for the students are as follows:

A. ORAL ACTIVITIES

(2) General discussion of the movie should be held to see whether or not the students enjoyed it, and clarify those parts they might have not understood.

(3) The students should be motivated to narrate the summary of the the movie . The teacher should skip around the class and asking each students to continue the narration of the plot in one or two sentences.

(4) The students can take the role of the movie' s protagonists and reenact specific scenes based on the movie.

(5) Some striking grammatical structures should be picked for open discussion and the students should be asked to produce some more sentences of the same pattern.

B. WRITTEN ACTIVITIES

(1) Movie Reviews: Students should write a movie review for another class or for a newsletter. either recommending the movie or saying why they would not recommend the people to see it.

(2) Students should select a scene from the movie they specially like and then rewrite the dialogue from the memory.

(3) Role Plays: Any of the role plays mentioned above can be written as a dialogue or as a short skit (in small group of students). The application of this approach will show very positive results in written classes. This will enrich the situations, thinking, and help them to express themselves creatively on the topics presented in the class.

REFERENCES

(1) Mac Lean , R.(1968) Television in Education , London. PP. 11-12

(2) Jack, Lonergan: (1984) Video in Language Learning, London , P. 1

(3) Wills , J (1983) "The Role of Visual Element in Spoken Discourse " in Video Application in Language teaching , ELT Document 114 England. P. 30

(4) Cole, R. (1931) Modern Foreign Language and Their Teaching. New York P.58

(5) Rivers, Wilga , M. (1968) Teaching Foreign Language Skills, London, Oxford University Press. P.18

(6) Noam, Chomsky. (1958) Congnitive process of learning, ELT Journal, Vol. 15 (3)2.

7. Widdowson, H. G. (1979) Teaching Language as Communication. Oxford University Press. P. 58

(8) Newmark,L. (1971) A Minimal Language Teaching Program, Cambridge University Press. P.25

(9) Winitz, H. (1975) Comprehension and Problem Solving Strategies for Language Training . Oxford University Press. London .p.89

(10) Balaaco, Simon. (1998) Comprehension, the Key to Second Language Acquisition. Cambridge University Press. P.55

CHAPTER-3

Speaking Skill and Media Technology

3.1 Speech is an innate and one of the most precious traits that the human beings are endowed with on this planet. Since childhood human beings have possessed immense desire to express their feelings, emotion, melancholy and happiness to their fellow beings in different languages. In fact their survival becomes meagre if they have least potential or no potential at all to speak. More so with English, this has now acquired distinct global position such as a link language, an international language of global business, a language of scholarship, a language of opportunity, a medium of instruction even in third world countries. In such global scenario if one acquires competence to communicate effectively in English he becomes more convincing, persuasive, and self assertive. Hence, speaking is at the heart of second language learning. It is arguably the most important skill for business and government personnel working in various fields. With the current state of global economies, effective presentation in English and public speaking skill are more important than ever. Your competence in persuading your audience to adopt your point of view makes your sales presentation more effective. The business world depends upon global communication, and being able deliver confident and authentic messages to your clients and shareholders is key to your success. Your speaking abilities in English have tremendous impact on your advancement and industry leadership. Your vision powerfully expressed imparts the bottom line and your company's success. Your powerful communication techniques will enhance your ability to persuade your customers. On the contrary a lack of communication in English means projects will fail, funding wouldn't be approved and careers will stall. Competence in public speaking improves growing public persona. Whether you are giving a formal speech or a quick presentation or simply anticipating a chance to offer an opinion during meeting, practicing in front of mirror can be invaluable. If a senior executive cannot communicate effectively at all levels their organization wouldn't be integrated into the business. In any profession growing your ability to speak and present effectively in English will reap huge rewards. How will boosting your communication skill grow your career and results? To get ahead, a chief information officer must be an effective communicator in English to gain support for their information technology programs and to advance in the organization. This is true for any technology professional or executive. In IT, poor communication in English is a common complaint from the rest of the business. Public speaking is one key component of critical communication skill and how people hear and respond to you. How you present yourself when you speak will mean the difference in succeeding or failing – not just with your budget and project success rate but with your staff and with your personal organization results. C.owing your public speaking means people listen and act when you talk. You create new opportunities for business and growth. It will increase your competitive and advantage and grow your career in new ways. Good speaking skill is an investment in yourself and your business.

There are two levels of communication in English; one is at the level of conversation. At this level the learner is able to converse and to communicate his needs and requirements. After systematic efforts for acquiring competence, the learner moves to English at competence level. Here he is able to communicate effectively leaving behind an indelible mark. He becomes more convincing, persuasive and self assertive with the choice of specific rhetorical diction and syntax. So far as the public speech is concerned there are numerous strategies to improve public speaking skill.

One can't acquire public speech competence overnight. It requires systematic practice. Those who are the beginners feel shy and hesitant to appear and speak in public. May be they have stage freight owing to poor ideas and language deficiency. But regular practice will be a miraculous panacea to overcome the aforesaid shortcomings.

3.1.1. How to improve Public Speaking

Before the speaker speaks in public he should write the speech and read it again and again until he is able to assimilate the whole speech in his mind in a systematic manner. Instead of thinking how he is going to survive this speech, he should think how he is going to deliver a fantastic speech. This will build up his self confidence to perform well in public speech. To establish a good dialogue and rapport with the audience and to motivate them to participate in the discussion will boost his self confidence. At the end of his speech he should offer question and answer session simply asking "***are there any questions? Or The floor is open for discussion***. And if finds it difficult to get people to ask questions the he needs ask some simplest questions. This may help break the ice and get people asking questions thereby giving the audience a chance to interact with the speaker and to gather more information on the ongoing discussion. According o **Sinha**[1] A little humor is also acceptable here to keep the discussion lively. This way the speaker will learn to enjoy himself while giving public speech. He will feel his confidence growing each time he gives a public presentation.

Monotonous style, monotonous tone, monotonous accent and monotonous voice are always boring for the audience. So one should change his voice every now and then during his speech. If he wants to emphasize the point, he should use his rhetorical voice. If he is trying to convey energy, anger, happiness, excitement or other emotion in his speech he should use his tone and voice accordingly.

Keeping context and situation in mind always makes the speech most suitable to the audience. The speaker should be sure to know the audience age, gender and interest so that he can modulate his speech, choose words and phrases accordingly.

3.1.2. Body Language

Speaker's body language is an important component to make the speech effective and convincing. He should make his facial expressions gestures, shrug and body movements, decent , appropriate, motivating and inspiring. The speaker should use eye contact when giving his speech. He should not focus on only one person in the room . But he should look around the room catching people's eyes so that each person in the audience feels he is speaking to them. He needs to make his opening to be catchy. This will be a good idea to open the discussion with an icebreaker such as asking the audience questions or telling a good joke. He can make his presentation more interesting by using audio and visual materials.

3.1.3. Using handouts as a tool for public speaking.

Handouts can be very important for effective public speaking. It makes it easier for the listeners to follow what one is discussing. If the speaker is going to use handouts he should be sure to choose the right time to give them out. He should not give them at the very beginning of his speech. Because this will distract the audience. By including handout he will be offering his listeners a way to remember what the speaker talked about and a way for them to reference back to certain aspects they want to remember at a later stage. The audience will appreciate his speech more if this service is offered.

There are other strategies to make the communication effective and worthwhile. Tremendous improvements will take place in one's communication skill if one follows the following guidelines: Good accent ,intonation , clear articulation, speed, loudness and voice modulation are the additional attributes of good speech. If one has motivation and eagerness one can acquire all these traits.

3.1.4. Speed

The speaker should be neither too fast nor too slow in his speech. The listeners cannot understand unduly fast speaker. Because they are most likely to miss some important links in the sequence resulting in confusion. On the other hand if the speaker is too slow he is most likely to make the speech boring. Speed should be conditioned to the situation. It could be adjusted according to the level of the audience. If the audience are properly qualified then one can speak a little faster. But, on the other hand if the audience have little or no knowledge of the subject then the speaker must speak slowly. Sometimes the level of intricacy of the subject determines the speed. The speaker must have the ability to judge for himself the speed at which he should speak on a particular occasion. When the speaker is addressing a large audience, he should be reasonably loud so that he is audible even to the people farthest from him. The speaker needs to adjust and modulate the volume of his sound according to the situation. This is so because a very loud speaker offends the audience, and a very soft speaker is likely to become unintelligible. A good speaker must therefore strike a balance between the two extremes.

3.1.5. Clear Articulation another important aspect of good speech is clear articulation. The first aim of the speaker is that he should be intelligible to the listeners. This aim is defeated the articulation is not clear. The sounds and syllables should be properly articulated. They should not be swallowed. Voice modulation should be maintained. Voice mudulation refers to the various changes in pitch or intonation. The pitch and intonation should vary according the situation. If the pitch remains constant, that is if one maintains a monotone the audience feels bored and soon become restive and inattentive. Pitch must be therefore lowered or raised according to the situation. The most important part of an utterance can be made to stand out from the rest if it is said on a relatively higher pitch just as the most important word in an utterance can be distinguished from the rest if a significant pitch movement is initiated on it. Strong motivation is the first precondition to acquire these attributes and to become an effective speaker. Once you acquire these attributes your speech will become more intelligible, more effective and more impressive.

3.2. PHONETICS AND SPOKEN ENGLISH

3.2.1. Phonetics:

The system of speech sounds of a language or a group of languages. Sound is produced by a number of co-coordinated articulatory activities such as voicing, tongue position, lip rounding and so on. Each of these activities is given the name of feature. For example. [p]

is composed of features like [labial] [+consonantal] [-continuant] etc. These features simply describe the place and the manner of articulation required for the articulation of the segment[p].

[P]

[+ Consonantal] this is one of the sets of features that distinguishes a consonant, from a vowel or a glide.

[- voice] this is one of the sets of laryngeal features that defines the state of the glottis.

[-voice] implies that the vocal cords are stiff and don't vibrate.

[Labial] this defines place of articulation when the lower lip touches the upper lip. Place of articulation involves the active and passive articulation used in the production of a particular consonant. Bilabial , labiodentals' and dental .Alveolar, post alveolar and palato alveola .Alveolar: palatal and velar

[-Continuant] This defines manner of articulation .e.g. [lateral], [nasal], [dela release] etc.

3.2.2. Manner of Articulation:

It includes the following points :

(1) Plosive : Simultaneous oral and nasal closure . Active and Passive articulators come in firm contact with each other . Soft palate is raised so as to shut off the nasal passage. The air behind the oral closure is compressed and then the air escapes with explosions. The following phonemes are the plosives: [P] , [b], [t] , [d], [k] , [g] etc.

[p] Voiceless bialabial plosive

(1) vocal cords are held a part.

(2) lips are in firm contact with each other.

(3) soft palate is raised and nasal passage is closed.

(4) stricture; complete closure and sudden release of the air.

[b] voiced bialabial plosive

(1) vocal cords vibrate.

(2) Lips are in firm contact.

(3) soft palate is raised

(4) complete closure of the air with sudden release.

[t] Voiceless alveolar plosive

(1) vocal cords are held a part. They don't vibrate

(2) the tip of the tongue makes a firm contact with the teeth ridge.

(3) soft palate is raised and nasal is shut .

(4) complete closure of the air with sudden release.

[d] Voiced alveolar plosive

(1) Vocal cords vibrate

(2) tip of the tongue comes in close contact with teeth ridge.

(3) soft palate is raised and nasal is shut.

(4) Complete closure of the air with sudden release.

[k] voiceless velar plosive

(1) vocal cords are held a part so they don't vibrate.

(2) back of the tongue touches the soft palate.

(3) soft palate is raised and nasal passage is shut.

(4) there is a complete closure of the air stream with sudden release.

[g] Voiced velar plosive

(1) Vocal cords vibrate.

(2) back of the tongue touches the soft palate.

(3) soft palate is raised and nasal passage is shut.

(4) Complete closure of the air with sudden release.

(2) Affricate : The air isn't held for any appreciable time but it is released slowly. E.g. /t/ and /d/

[tʃ] Voiceless palato alveolar affricate

(1) vocal cords don't vibrate.

(2) Tip of the tongue touches the teeth ridge.

(3) The air is released slowly.

/d/ voiced palato alveolar

(1) vocal cords vibrate

(2) front part of the tongue touches the teeth ridge.

(3) Air is released slowly.

(3) Fricative : Active and passive articulators make a firm contact. Passage between them is very narrow and the air passes through it with audible friction . E.g. [f]. [v], [θ] , [ð] ,[s] , [z] , [ʃ] , [3]

[f] voiceless labiodental fricative

(1) vocal cords don't vibrate.

(2) lower lip makes contact with upper teeth.

(3) air is released slowly causing friction .

[V] voiced labio dental fricative

(1) vocal cords vibrate.

(2) lower lip makes contact with upper teeth.

(3) air is released slowly causing friction

[θ] Voiceless dental fricative

(1) vocal cords don't vibrate

(2) tip of the tongue touches the upper front teeth.

(3) air is released slowly causing friction

[ð] voiced dental fricative

(1) vocal cords vibrate

(2) tip of the tongue touches the upper front teeth.

(3) air is released slowly causing friction.

[s] Voiceless alveolar plosive

(1) vocal cords don't vibrate

(2) tip of the tongue touches teeth ridge.

(3) air is released slowly causing friction

[z] voiced alveolar plosive

(1) vocal cords vibrate

(2) tip of the tongue touches the teeth ridge.

(3) air is released slowly causing friction.

[ʃ] voiceless palato alveolar fricative

(1) vocal cords don't vibrate

(2) tip of the tongue comes in contact with back of the teeth ridge.

(3) Air is released causing friction.

[ʒ] voiced palato alveolar fricative

(1) vocal cords vibrate.

(2) tip of the tongue comes in contact with teeth ridge.

(3) air is released slowly causing friction .

[h] voiceless glottal fricative

(1) vocal cords don't vibrate

(2) sound is produced by glottis.

(3) air is released slowly causing friction.

(4) Nasal: complete closure of oral passage. No closure of nasal passage. The soft palate is lowered and the air passes through the nose. E.g. [m] ,[n]

[m] voiced bialabial nasal

(1) vocal cords vibrate.

(2) lower lips make firm contact with upper teeth.

(3) complete oral closure.

(4) soft palate is lowered so the air passes through nose.

[n] voiced alveolar nasal

(1) vocal cords vibrate.

(2) tip of the tongue touches the teeth ridge

(3) complete oral closure, soft palate is lowered , so the air passes through nose.

(5) Lateral: A stricture of closure in the centre of the vocal tract but the air has a free passage on the sides. E.g. [l]

[l] Voiced alveolar Lateral

(1) tip of the tongue makes a firm contact with alveolar ridge.

(2) complete closure along the centre of the oral tract.

(3) soft palate is raised ,nasal passage is shut.

A lateral consonant is articulated with a stricture of complete closure in the Centre of the vocal tract. The sides of the tongue are lowered and the air escapes along the sides of the mouth.

[r] a voiced post alveolar frictionless continuant.

(1) Vocal cords vibrate.

(2) The tip of the tongue is raised in the direction of the teeth ridge

(3) soft palate is raised so as to shut off the nasal passage of air. The air from the lungs come out of the space between the tip of the tongue and the post alveolar region without any friction. [r] is a vowel like in its articulation but it is classified under consonant because they always occur in the marginal position in syllables.

Semi Vowels : a vowel glide to a more prominent sound in the same syllable.

In English there are two semi vowels. E.g. [j] and [w] .

[j] unrounded voiced palatal semi vowels

Soft palate is raised so as to shut off the nasal passage of the air. The front of the tongue assumes a position for a vowel between close and half close and quickly glides to the position of the following vowels. The vocal cords vibrate producing voice. The lips are neutral or spread during the articulation of [j] .

(6) Trill: (rolled consonant) Active articulator taps several times against the passive articulators . Tip of the tongue strikes against the teeth ridge a number of times.

(7) Flap: active articulator strikes against the passive articulators once only.

Syllable: is a part of a word that contains a single vowel-sound and that is pronounced as a unit. So, for example, "book" has one syllable, and "reading" has two syllables .

Rhythm: It occurs when stressed syllables tend to occur at regular intervals of time. Stressed syllable should be pronounced carefully and the unstressed one should be crowded together and said quickly. It is this regular occurrence of stressed syllables that gives English its characteristic rhythm

Stress : A degree of prominence a syllable has.It is an emphasis that you put on a word or a part of a word when you pronounce it so that it sounds slightly louder.

E.g. after***Noon***, ciga***Rette***, repre***Sent***

Primary stress is on the last syllable and the secondary stress is on the first syllable

3.3 FUNCTIONAL SHIFT OF STRESS

According to **Gimson**[2] there are a number of words of two syllables in which the accentual pattern depends on whether the word is used as a noun , an verb or a verb. When the word is used as a noun or an adjective the stress is on the first syllable.

When the word is used as a verb the stress is on the second syllable. E.g.

Noun/Adj	Verb	Noun/Adj	Verb
Absent	Absent	progress	Progress
Object	Object	Prodece	Produce
Subject	Subject	Perfect	Perfect
Permit	Permit	Increase	Increase
Record	Record	Decrease	Decrease

Words With Prefixes / suffixes and Their Stress Patterns

(1) Words with weak prefixes are accented on the root.

arise behold aloud apart become

befall begin

(2) Prefixes with negative connotation get stressed . E.g.

disloyal illogical halffinished

(3) Verbs of two syllables beginning with prefix (dis) are stressed or the last syllable . E.g.

disarm dismay disclose dismiss disgrace

Disguise disturb

(4) Verbs of two syllables ending in – ate , — ise, —— ize, —— ct are stressed on the last syllable.

narrate debate migrate vibrate capsize
attract depict connect infect chastise
comprise

(5) **Words ending in – ion have the stress on the penultimate (1e.thelast but one) syllable.**

application civilization imagination cultivation

(6) **Words ending in –ic , - ical , - ically , - ial , - ially , ian have Stress on the syllable preceding the suffix.**

- **- ic** = apologetic, electric, patriotic, scientific
- **- ical** = apologetical
- **- ically** = apologetically
- **- ial** = memorial, presidential
- **- ian** = musician, politician, victorian, electrician

(7) **Words ending in – ious , eous , have the stress on the penultimate (i.e.the last but one syllable)**

- ious = anxious, injurious, laborious, victorious

(8) **Words ending in ' ity" have stress on the anti-penultimate syllable (ie. Third from the end)**

ity = ability, activity curiosity

(9) **Words ending in " – cracy, - crat" have the stress on the anti-penultimate syllable (third from the end)**

democracy aristocracy democrat technocrat

(10) **Words ending in – graph - graphy , - meter , - logy have stress on the anti- penultimate (third from the end)**

paragraph, Photograph, Photography, biography, parameter, thermometer, psychology, biology, zoology

(11) **Words ending with the suffixes have the stress on the suffixes . E.g**

_ ain obtain, pertain, explain, retain

· aire millionaire, questionnaire,

eer	**engineer,**	**career,**
ental	**experimental,**	fundamental
ee	**payee,**	employee

(12) Accent on the Compound Words

Most compound words have the primary stress on the first element. For example:

Blacksmith **black**bird **tea**party

(13) Accent on the second syllable in such compound words, such as:

however	him**self**	**herself**	your**self**	my**self**
themselves	after**noon**	**oldfashioned**	absent**minded**	

(14) Stress Shift

academy	**academic**	acade**mi**cian
photography	**photographer**	photography
politics	**poli**tical	politician

3.4 SILENT CONSONANT LETTERS

According to **J. Sethi**[3] Silent consonant letters constitute one of the problem areas in respect of pronunciation of English words. To solve some of the problems of learners, a few spelling sequences containing silent letters are discussed below:

(I) / b/ is always silent in the spelling sequences / mb / and / bt / occurring in the word final position:

Comb, numb, bomb, limb, debt

Lamb, thumb, womb, climb, doubt

Tomb, succumb, plumb

Note: / b / is always silent in plumber , bomber , subtle etc

(II) / d/ is always silent in the spelling sequence /dj /

Adjective, adjunct, adjacent

Adjudge, adjoin, adjutant

Adjourn, adjust, adjudicate

(III) / g / is silent in the spelling system / gm / or / gn /

Phlegm, paradigm, gnarl, gnash

Poignant, gnaw, physiognomy, sign

Resign, assign, consign, malign

Campaign

Note: however / g/ is not silent in the following words

e. g phlegmatic, paradigmatic, signature

resignation, malignant

(IV) / h / is silent in the spelling sequence / gh/ and in the word final position :

Ghost, aghast, ghastly, ghetto

Note : / h / is also silent in John, Thames, Thomas.

(V) / k / is always silent in the word-initial spelling sequence / kn / :

Kneel, knob, knave, knife

Knee, knight, knowledge, knock

(VI) / l / is silent before / k / and / m/ in the word final spelling

sequences **l** and **lm** in some words such as the following :

walk, talk, stalk, folk

balm, palm, psalm, calm

(VII) / n / is silent in the word-final spelling sequence / mn / :

Autumn, column, condemn, damn

Hymn, solemn, calm

Note : However, / n / is not silent in derivatives formed from such words .

Examples : autumnal, condemnable, damnable

Hymnal, solemnity

(IX) / p / is silent in the word – initial spelling sequences / pn/ , / ps /

and / pt/ :

Pneumonia, psalm, Ptolemy

Psychology, pseudonym, psyche

(X) / w / is silent in the (a) final position, (b) initial spelling sequence wr, and (c) sometimes initial spelling sequences wh :

Saw, raw, claw, flow, snow, show

Wreath, writhe, write, wring, wrest, wrestle

Wrist, wreck, wrap

Who, whom, whose, whole, whoop, whore

3.5 PRONOUNCIATION OF SUFFIXES

According to **Christophersen**[4] Suffixes used for making plurals and possessives of nouns and simple present tense, third person singular from verbs are pronounced / s / , /z/

/ iz / . Though these suffixes are always represented by the letter / s / Or the letter /es / . the pronunciation of these suffixes are governed by The following rules.

(1) These suffixes are pronounced / s /
after voiceless consonant other than / s / , / ʃ / , /tʃ /

Cats	/ k χts/,	cook	/ kuks/,
cups	/ kʌps/ ,	month	mʌnθs

(2) They are pronounced / z / after voiced sounds (voiced sounds include vowels other than / d3 / , / z / , / 3 /

bags	/ bχgz /	birds	/ b3:d z /
calls	kɒlz	cities	siti:z
comes	kʌmz	cows	kauz
goes	gəuz	loves	lʌvz
plays	pleiz	rubs	rʌbz
sons	sʌnz	calls	

(3) They are pronounced / iz / when the root (singular noun or infinite form of the verbs end in / s / , / z / , / 3 / , / tʃ / and / d3 /.

Buses	**/ b ʌsiz / ,**	**bushes**	**/buʃiz /**
Catches	**/ k χ tʃiz /**	**edges**	**/ edʒiz /**
Garage	**/ gχra:d3iz /**	**roses**	**/ rəuziz /**

REFERENCES

(1) Sinha,K.K . (2002) Business Communication, Galgotia Publishing Company, Karol Bagh, New Delhi.

(2) Gimson.A.C. (1967) English Pronunciation Practice. London, University of London Press.

(3) Sethi,J. (2008) A Practical Course in English Pronunciation, PHI Learning Private Limited.

(4) Christophersen, P. (1956) An English Phonetic Course. London, Longmans.

CHAPTER-4

VOCABULARY AND SPEAKING SKILL

4.1.1. HOW TO IMPROVE VOCABULARY

One of the major obstacles to the fast acquisition of communication skills is the learner's poor vocabulary. The novice non-native users of English for their being less exposed to English language have poor vocabulary so they manifest their inability to decipher the writer's intended meaning in the given text. They cannot speak or write with ease. There is no doubt that the knowledge of substantial vocabulary assists the learner's proficiency in all the integrated skills but it is quite ironical that the vocabulary teaching which is a key to success in the development of language skills has always been given a short shrift in the class. It has been taken up in a haphazard manner. No attempt has ever been made to adopt effective strategies for vocabulary teaching. The development of vocabulary mostly relies on the learner's special interest. So only enthusiastic learners who have implicit motivation usually make extensive reading of novels in order to enrich their vocabulary. On the contrary less motivated students remain handicapped. The basic reason for the student's lack of motivation is that the vocabulary teaching has neither been a part of curriculum nor the preoccupation of the teacher. Therefore the focus should be laid on vocabulary teaching which is quite significant for promoting communication skill Another widely acknowledged way to build vocabulary is through the teaching of word-formation process sometimes called "derivational morphology". A word is easily understood with reference to its derivational process. More so, many words when analyzed into their constituent parts yield their own definition. Such analysis of word formation is the model of generative vocabulary which is really a short cut for vocabulary development. Certain basic principles for the teaching of generative vocabulary are as follows:

(1) Learning to look analytically at word form.

(2) Recognizing the underlying stem through the knowledge of affixation.

(3) Discovering the meaning of the whole by analyzing the parts.

(4) Discovering the meaning of strange words by establishing meaningful association.

So the learner can at least get the import of the difficult words if the study of root-affix elements is undertaken. First the teacher should take initiative to analyze and dissect the combination of these elements in the class. Then the students should be given numerous words for practice. Thus a systematic study of their roots and their etymology would enable the learner to make practical association between the root and the added words and hence enrich the learner's range of vocabulary.

4.1.2. A systematic way of developing vocabulary includes words in a variety of ways and presenting them through various types of tasks and games. According to **Norman Lewis**[5] there are several ways of putting words in groups: collocation, word network , synonyms and antonyms . Collocation is an interesting feature of language. In English certain words go together and it does not make sense to collocate or put together certain other words. In other word, collocation is a frequent co-occurrence of certain words such as distant relative, remote area, strong tea etc.

Hyponymy: The teacher should teach the students how to group together words which belong to some parent words or which fall under some specific domain such as:

Stationary : pen, pencil, ink, paper

The teacher should express this sense relation by saying that stationary is the super-ordinate word and pen , pencil and ink are hyponyms of stationary. To collect words of some specific domain also builds up an extensive vocabulary such as the words that describe all kinds of people or the words that are related to medical specialists such as:

Egoist = self seeker

Altruist = generous, benevolent

Introvert = self centered, reclusive

Extrovert = extremely sociable

Ambivert = neither extreme

Medical Specialists: a gynaecologist, an obstertrician, an ophthalmologist, an orthopaedist, cardiologist, a neurologist etc.

If such vocabulary listing of various streams is undertaken in the class it will yield successful result and equip the learners with the words of varied streams. If frequent occurrence of long words in scientific texts is a major problems for the students of science. They can not understand the meanings of such formidable words. To overcome this problem, the teacher should simplify the long words by breaking them into prefixes, suffixes and roots. There is no doubt that lexicons are relatively long but their length no bar to their understanding if their constituents are analyzed separately. Once these constituents have been mastered they become self explanatory and hence there is no difficulty in discovering the meanings of such long words.

4.1.3 One Word Substitution

Match the sentences with one word Substitution

Sentences	Meaning
(1) People of noble families or the highest social class. ( )	(a) **Ambiguity**
(2) A person who doesn't believe in God . ( )	(b) **Aristocracy**
(3) **An** expression or statement having more than one meaning ( )	(C) **Atheist**
(4) An account of somebody's life written by that person ( )	(d) **Biography**
(5) An account of somebody's life written by another person ( )	(e) **Autobiography**
(6) somebody who eats human flesh ( )	(f) **Soporific**
(7) somebody who works or serves only for personal profit ( )	(g) **Misogamist**
(8) a person who hates women ( )	(h) **Mercenary**
(9) a person who does not believe in the institution of marriage ( )	(i) **Misogynist**
(10) a drug or other substance that induces sleep ( )	(j) **Cannibal**

Answers : (1) b (2) c(3) a (4) e (5) d (6) j (7) h (8) i (9) g (10) f

Sentences	**Meaning**
(1) a person who knows everything. ( )	(a) **Impervious**
(2) a person who has power over all ( )	(b) **Fanatic**
(3) a supposed cure for all diseases or problems ( )	(C) **Infallible**
(4) a person who remains unmoved by other people's opinions ( )	(d) **feminist**
(5) incapable of making a mistake ( )	(e) **Panacea**
(6) the worship of idols or false gods ( )	(f) **Inflammable**
(7) something that is easily set on fire and burned ( )	(g) **Omniscient:**
(8) somebody who is dedicated to sensual pleasure and luxury ( )	(h) **Omnipotent:**
(9) one who has extreme beliefs, in religion or politics ( )	(i) **Idolatry**
(10) a believer in women's rights. ( )	(j) **Epicure**

Answer: (1) g (2) h (3) e (4) a (5) c (6) I (7) f (8) j (9) b (10) d

Sentences	Meaning
(1) the crime in which somebody kills his or her own brother ( )	(a) Patricide
(2) the act of murdering one's own mother ( )	(b) Fratricide
(3) the act of murdering one's own father ( )	(c) Anarchist
(4) a person who rejects a system of government ( )	(d)Ambidextrous
(5) a person who is able to use both hands with equal skill ( )	(e) Matricide
(6) financial support to ex-wife ( )	(f) Autocracy
(7)a person who does something for pleasure rather than for pay ( )	(g) Alimony
(8) rule by one person who holds unlimited power ( )	(h) Potable
(9) fit for eating ( )	(i) Edible
(10) fit for drinking ( )	(j) Amateur

Answer: (1) b (2) e (3) a (4) c (5) d (6) g (7) j (8) f (9) i (10) h

Sentences	Meaning
(1) nations engaged in war ( )	(a) Fastidious
(2) one who is concerned that even the smallest details be just right ( )	(b) Belligerents
(3) sleepwalking ( )	(C) Stoic
(4) a person who is unaffected by emotions ( )	(d)Somnambulism
(5) a person who believes in the existence of God ( )	(e) Verbatim
(6) corresponding word for word translation ( )	(f) Theist
(7) take legal action against somebody ( )	(g) Pugnacity
(8) inclined to fight or be aggressive ( )	(h) Prosecute
(9) having more than one spouse at the same time ( )	(i) Polyandry
(10) the custom of having more than one husband at the same time	(j) Polygamy

Answers : (1) b (2) a (3) d (4) c (5) f (6) e (7) h (8) g (9) j (10) I

4.1.4. QUIZ ON SOME BUSINESS AND LEGAL TERMINOLOGIES

(1) solicitor

A type of lawyer in Britain and Australia who is trained to prepare cases and give legal advice. A solicitor does not normally speak in court.

(2) beneficiary

This is a person of company that actually owns money or other property, that is held by someone else for their benefit. For example: If a company gives money to a parent on behalf of a child, the child is the beneficiary.

(3) Court: A "court" is the building where trials happen.

(4) patent

Like a copyright or a trademark, a patent is a legal device to protect IP (Intellectual Property.) Patents are designed to protect inventions.

(a)	**Eight men arrested in anti-terror raids two weeks ago appeared in __________ on Wednesday charged with conspiracy to murder.**
(b)	**A Fenland firm which makes pill coatings has been granted a __________ for a new type of capsule.**
(c)	**Any money left over can be claimed by the __________.**
He returned the papers to my __________ straight away...	

Answers : (a) court (b) patent (c) beneficiary (d) solicitor

(5) case

A case is a trial that has been completed and recorded.

(6) accuse

To "accuse" someone is to state that they have done something wrong, illegal or unkind. C.f. "to charge" (To be formally accused of a crime by the police.

(7) witness

A person who gives evidence in Court.

(8) common law

Rules of law based on previous court decisions.

(a) __________ said the truck was going too fast to make the sharp turn.
(b) It is a criminal act under __________ to assist with a suicide.
(c) Sexual assault __________ overturned"
(d) Police __________ teenager of bringing gun to school"

Answer : (a) witness (b) common law (c) case (d) accuse

(9) offence

An offence is a illegal act, a crime.

(10) breach

When one party breaks the terms of a contract.

(11) plaintiff

The person who brings an case to court. Also known as the "claimant"

(12) IP

IP (Intellectual Property) covers ideas, inventions and other creations that are given protection from copying under law. The forms of protection include copyright, patents and trademarks.

1. **The first case was decided in favour of the ___**
2. **Protecting __________ is a way of encouraging more investment, research and innovation.**
3. **Sanders responded in January by suing SLA for __________ of contract.**
4. **Each __________, if proven, may result in a fine of up to £2,500.**

Answers: (a) plaintiff (b) IP (c) breach (d) offence

(13) overturn

To "overturn" the decision of a court means to invalidate or reverse it.

(14) exchange

When contracts are "exchanged" the parties become legally bound by it.

(15) bound

To be "bound" means to have your actions restricted by a legal limit.

(16) copyright

Copyright is parts by the Copyright, Designs and Patent Act 1988 and is a law designed to protect the intellectual property of the creators of original work, for example authors, musicians and computer programmers.

(a) Government lawyers argued President Bush was not __________ by laws banning torture.

(b) The makers of the hit television show Pop Idol" are suing a Peruvian television company, accusing it of violating their __________.

(c) "Microsoft fails to __________ court ruling."

(d) When you __________ contracts you are legally obliged to proceed with the transaction.

Answers: (a) bound (b) copyright (c) overturn (d) exchange

(17) receivership

Once a company has been declared bankrupt control is given to a "receiver" who will dispose of the assets and close the company down. When this occurs, the company is said to be in "receivership".

(18) injunction

An \njunction" is a ruling by a court that stops a company or a person doing something.

(19) adjourn

To put off, postpone or discontinue until another time.

(20) damages

An amount of money awarded by a court as compensation for loss or injury.

(a) Judge George Maluleke agreed to __________ the case to allow Scott-Crossley to consult a doctor.
(b) The family of a deceased smoker has been awarded $2 million in __________.
(c) Star Holdings Ltd has gone into __________ owing between $1 million and $2 million
(d) EarthLink is asking the court to issue an __________ preventing the defendants from "illegally spamming

Answers : (a) adjourn (b) damages (c) receivership (d) injunction

(21) guilty

If a court finds a defendant "guilty" they have decided that he or she committed the crime. C.f. "not guilty"

(22) pleaded

A defendant's reply to a charge put to him by a court; can be "guilty" or "not guilty". Also verb: "to plead"

(23) ex gratia

In British law, the Latin term "ex gratia" means "out of kindness, voluntary."

(24)ruling

A "ruling" is a decision made by a court.

(a) The __________ payment of £1,000 is intended to cover the expenses incurred as a result of the fire.	
(b) Crosoft argued that he court __________ would have "dangerous repercussions" for small software developers.	
(c) Teenager Luke Mitchell has been found __________ of the murder of his girlfriend Jodi Jones.	
(d) These accountants __ guilty to fraud.	

Answers : (a) ex-gratia (b) ruling (c) guilty (d) pleaded

(25) Sentence

The punishment ordered by a court for a defendant convicted of a crime.

(26) dismissed

A "dismissal" is a decision made my the court that a claim is not valid and that proceedings should end. A case is "dismissed".

(27) accomplice

A partner in a crime.

(28) agent

An agent is a person who is legally authorised to carry out activities on behalf of another.

(a) ---------- of convicted murderer was reduced
(b) He failed in his attempt to get the case _______last October
(c) Robert Williams is accused of being an __________ In Vernon Parker's murder of Valerie Spears.
(d) They are buying ________ to give my house key to the prospective buyers?

Answers : (a) sentence (b) dismissed (c) accomplice (d) agent

(29) misrepresentation

When two parties enter a contract, "misrepresentation" occurs if one party makes a false statement of fact to the other.

(30) copyright

Copyright is parts by the Copyright, Designs and Patent Act 1988 and is a law designed to protect the intellectual property of the creators of original work, for example authors, musicians and computer programmers.

(31) summons

An order to appear in court or to produce evidence to a court.

(32) witness

A person who gives evidence in Court.

(a) Jonathan Rand is resisting a __________ to give evidence before the court...
(b)A __________ said the truck was going too fast to make the sharp turn.
(a) ______ makes a contract voidable and may give rise to a damages claim.
(b) The makers of the hit television show Pop Idol" are suing a Peruvian television company, accusing it of violating their ______

Answers: (a) summons (b) witness (c) misrepresentation (d) copyright

(33) icon: An icon is a small graphic representing a file or a program.

(34) font: A font is a set of print or display characters with a specific style and size.

(35) blogs: A blog is an online diary, someone who keeps a blog is a "blogger."

(36) router: A router is a device that transfers data from one network to another.

(a) To start Dr Watson double-click on its __________ in your system
(b) He says it must be typed and double-spaced, using 12 point __________
(c) Political _______ experienced huge popularity in the run up to the US presidential election
(d) A similar problem occurs with office users, who will often access to the US presidential election __________

Answers : icon (b) font (c) blogs (d) router

(37) hack: To hack means to write computer code at a very basic level, sometimes for illegal purposes. A person who hacks is called a hacker.

(38) bandwidth: In computer networks, bandwidth describes the amount of data that can be carried from one point to another within a particular time period. Bandwidth is usually expressed as "bit" per "second" or " bps".

(39) database: A database is a collection of data organized so that it can easily be accessed, managed and updated.

(40) URL: Uniform Resource Locator. A name that uniquely identifies a document or service on the Internet.

(a) MySQL is the __________ most frequently used to store data for websites written in PHP.
(b) We recommend Mac users type in the __________ http://www.poetrysociety.org.uk to access this website..
(c) Despite the constant scare stories, it's really very difficult for someone else on the Internet to __________ into your PC.
(d) The __________ size required for even a small web cast Substantial and extremely costly.

Answers: (a) database (b) URL (c) hack (d) bandwidth

(41) codec: A Codec is a technology used to compress or decompress data (usually video). Popular codecs include MPEG2 for digital video and MP3 for digital music.

(42) browser: Browser is a program that is used to look at webpages on the Internet.

(43) blogs: A blog is an online diary, someone who keeps a blog is a "blogger."

(44) LAN: A LAN (Local Area Network) is a network of computers and printers spread over a small area such as an office.

(a) RealAudio, a streaming file format, uses its own proprietary ___________, and requires the RealPlayer or NetShow to hear it.
(b) Please click "refresh" on your ___________ to view the most recent version of this story.
(c) Political ___________ experienced huge popularity in the run-up to the US presidential election.
(d) A NAT server acts as a connection point between your local ___________ and the Internet.

Answers : (a) codec (b) browser (c) blogs (d) Lan

(45) Linux: Linux is an open-source operating system for PCs based on the operating system used by UNIX computers.

(46) interface: A user communicates with an application through the "interface"

(46) FTP: (File Transfer Protocol) is a set of rules used for transferring files between computers on the Internet.

(47) virus : A software application, often installed on a computer without the owner's permission, that causes damage to that computer.

(a) PageMill 2.0 lacks an automatic method to ___________ all your files to a server
(b) The Nimda computer ___________ spread quickly around the World.
(c) The operating system ___________ now runs on most computer platforms including Intel, PowerPC and Sparc.
(d) When you first start Outlook Express, you'll see that there have been some changes made to the ___________...

Answer: (a) FTP(b) virus (c) linex (d) interface

4.1.5 : Synonyms and Antonyms

Words	Meanings	Words	Meanings
abbreviate	abridge, shorten	general	universal
abstan	refrain	gentle	tender, mild, kind
absurd	ridiculous	gigantic	huge, stupendous
accomplish	achieve, perform	giggle	laugh, titter
adversity	calamity, misfortune	grave	sober, serious
adversary	opponent, enemy	grief	sorrow, pain, agony
alteration	change	guard	defend, protect
amusement	recreation	habit	custom, practice
anger	ire, wrath, rage	hasty	rash
ascend	rise, soar, climb	hazardous	risky
authentic	genuine	heave	lift, raise
autocrat	despot, tyrant	hideous	repulsive, ugly
avaricious	greedy	hinder –	obstruct, prevent
aversion	dislike, antipathy	holy	sacred
brisk	vigorous	humble	meek
restrain,	stop, curb	idle	lazy, indolent
comprehend	understand, grasp	illegal	unlawful, lawless
confer	grant	impudent	impertinent
confess	admit	include	comprise
confuse	confound, perplex	increase –	enlarge, augment
contemplate	meditate	irritation	annoyance
contrary	opposite	jeer	mock, sneer
courteous	polite, civil	just	fair, impartial
degeneration	deterioration	juvenile	youthful
deplorable	regrettable, lamentable	keen	sharp
despise	scorn, disdain	obscene	filthy
dexterous	clever, skilful	obstacle	hindrance
dismal	gloomy	obstinate	stubborn
dizzy	giddy, dazed, unsteady	pardon	forgive, excuse
eccentric	peculiar, odd	pious	devout, godly, religious
efficient	able, competent	precise	exact
enormous	huge, immense	premature	hasty
eternal	timeless, perpetual	proficient	adept, expert
famous	celebrated, renowned	profuse	lavish, extravagant
felicity	happiness, bliss	progeny	offspring,
ferocious	fierce, savage	prudent	discreet, wise, sagacious
foolish	silly, stupid	revenge	vengeance, retribution
frailty	weakness, failing, foible	rude	impolite, discourteous
frank	candid, open	superfluous	unnecessary, needless
reverence	reverence – veneration	vanquish	conquer, defeat
thrifty	frugal, economical	winsome	charming, attractive
vulgar	coarse, indecent		

ANTONUMS

Antonyms are words of the same grammatical class that have opposite meanings. A list of antonyms is given below. For a comprehensive list, consult a good thesaurus.

Words	Antonyms	Words	Antonyms
common	rare	famous	obscure
compulsory	optional	fast	loose, slow
concord	discord	fat	lean, thin
confident	diffident	fictitious	real
create	destroy	forget	remember
dark	light	frequent	rare
dawn	dusk	fresh	stale
debtor	creditor	full	empty
deep	shallow	gain	loss
defensive	offensive	gather	scatter
deliberate	unintentional	general	particular, special
diligent	crazy	generous	mean
dilute	concentrated	gradual	abrupt, sudden
dwarf	giant	guilty	innocent
elevation	depression	harsh	gentle
exclude	include	hasty	leisurely
exit	entrance	hate	love
exotic	indigenous	haughty	meek
expand	contract	heavy	light
explicit	implicit	high	low
external	internal	hit	miss
extravagant	frugal, thrifty	hollow	solid
hurt	heal	honour	shame
ideal	actual	hope	despair
idle	busy	host	guest
imagination	reality	lament	rejoice
increase	decrease	later	earlier
industrious	indolent, lazy	latter	former
inferior	superior	lead	follow
inhale	exhale	lend	borrow
input	output	let	hire
joy	sorrow	liberate	enslave
junior	senior	literal	figurative
kind	cruel	loose	tight
kindle	extinguish	lose	find

knowledge	ignorance	major	minor
material	spiritual	many	few
maximum	minimum	masculine	feminine
memory	oblivion	practice	theory
mild	severe, stern	pragmatic	idealistic
miser	spendthrift	praise	blame
monogamy	polygamy	precede	succeed
monotony	variety,	pride	humility
naïve	sophisticated	profit	loss
narrow	broad	progress	regress
native	foreign	progressive	retrograde
natural	artificial	promote	demote
negative	positive	public	private
neutral	partial	quiet	noisy
observe	reverse	queer	normal
odd	even	rash	cautious, careful
offer	refuse	rapid	slow, leisurely
often	seldom	recede	advance
omission	commission	relative	absolute
optimistic	pessimistic	reluctant	ready, willing
oral	written	reserved	sociable
oriental	occidental	resist	submit
original	duplicate, copy	retail	wholesale
ostensible	actual	reward	punish

4.2 IDIOMS AND PHRASES

Idioms and phrases add color to the language. They serve as ornaments thereby making the language more beautiful and fascinating. According to Collins Cobuild English Language Dictionary " 6An idiom is a group of words which, when they are used together in a particular combination , have a different meaning from the one they would have if you took the meaning of all the individual words in the group". If one learns maximum number of idioms and phrases one is most likely to acquire competence in the language. The knowledge of idioms and phrases help learners understand the speaker, the book or any idioms-laden business correspondence. This also improves learners' competence in the language and makes their communication convincing and effective. It enables them to speak with felicity and ease. I have collected these idioms from different sources so that the learner can learn them and improve their ability to speak and write effectively.

The Cambridge International Dictionary of Idioms explains over 7,000 idioms current in British, American and Australian English on internet. They are helping helping learners to understand them and to use them with confidence. The Cambridge Dictionary of American idioms based on the 200 million words of American English text in the Cambridge International corpus, unlocks the meaning of more than 5,000 idiomatic phrases used in contemporary American English. I have also given full sentence examples to show how idioms are really used. Some of them are collected from Google search on internet.

(1) You have to raise your voice a little when talking to him. He's a little **hard of hearing.**

(a) Stubborn (b) quiet when he speaks

(c) deaf (d) distracted

(2) I went to a real nice restaurant yesterday. The food cost was cheap and they served a lot of food. I had to ask for a **doggy bag** because I couldn't eat the whole thing.

(a) package to store left over food so the person can take it home

(b) dog bowl so you can give the rest of the food to your dog.

(c) Special order where you get smaller meal size.

(d) Kid's meal

(3) Fabian was a **doormat.** No wonder his classmates were always giving him a hard time.

(a) snob (b) geek

(c) coward (d) chubby face

(1) I invited a friend to go to a street market by my house where they served some real good Japanese food. My

friend's mom wanted to pay for her daughter's meal, but I insisted opaying for both our meals myself, her mom finally said: Ok, as long as we **go Dutch** next time.

(a) I pay for your meal

(b) You take me with you

(c) you let me drive you there

(d) we divide the costs

(5) So, is everything **plain as a pikestaff**? Oh, yes indeed sir!

(a) clean (b) clear

(c) messy (d) in position

(6) We are having a **pot-luck dinner** at Tim's house tomorrow. Everybody is invited!

(a) dinner where everybody brings something to eat.

(b) Dinner where everybody chips in

(c) Dinner where only soap is served

(d) Dinner where people eat and play games at the same time

(7) I need everybody's help. The wedding is tomorrow and we haven't even started with the decorations yet. We have **no time to lose**.

(a) been procrastinating

(b) to remember what time it is

(c) extra time

(d) to start right now

(8) Just **keep your wig on**. Everything is going to be alright, okay?

(a) hold your wig so it won't fall off

(b) get another hair cut

(c) calm down

(d) throw a fit

(9) Kyle was **saved by the bell** when his sister walked in and asked him to take her to ballet practice.

(a) rescued from an unwanted situation

(b) detained from his duty

(c) obligated to comply

(d) obliged to cooperate

Answers : **(1) c (2) a (3) b (4) d (5) b (6) a** (7) d **(8) c (9) a**

COMMON IDIOMS AND PHRASES

(1) **come about** - happen : Nobody knows how these things came out.

(2) **come across** - find by accident : On my way to market I came across an old beggar.

(3) **Come upon** - to find by accident : While reading complaints, across such allegation.

(4) **come of** - to have as a result : What came of the discussion

(5) **come off** — happen , take place : The prize distribution ceremony will Come off next week.

(6) **Come to** - agree : you should come to terms with these organization

Idioms derived from parts of the body

(7) **Keep at arms length** —— to avoid being too friendly : He is very quarrelsome, So I keep him at arms length.

(8) **with open arms** - with great affection and enthusiasm. I welcomed my friend with open arms .

(9) **Break the back of something** - finish the hardest part of a work : Since my colleagues had already broken the back of it I could it easily.

(10) **put one's back into something** - work at something with all one's energy.

(11) **To put someone's back up** - make a person angry: His offensive manner put my back up

(11) **Be on somebody's back** - keep criticizing someone : He is still on my back about those ten pounds he lent me.

(12) **To stab somebody in the back** - to do something harmful to someone who trusted you : He was stabbed in the back by people he thought were his friends.

(13) **Turn your back on somebody** : refuse to help someone : I appealed for help, but they turned their back on me.

(14) **Be out of your brain (be very drunk)**

e.g. When he reached home last night, he was out of his brain.

(15) **Get your brain in gear** (make yourself start thinking clearly and effectively) e.g. I have got an important meeting today, so I have to get my brain in gear.

(16) **Rack your brain/brains** (think very hard, usually in order to remember something or to find a solution to a problem)

e.g. I've been racking my brains but I still can't find a solution to this vexed problem.

(17) **Turn the other cheek** (if you turn the other cheek, you don't get angry when someone attacks or insults you)

e.g Non-violence policy requires that you turn the other cheek, when someone hits you.

(18) **Keep/play your cards close to your chest** (not tell anyone what you plan to do) You will never know what he is going to do next. He plays his cards close to his chest.

(19) **Get it off your chest** (tell someone about something that has been worrying you) If you have a problem, get it off your chest and you will feel better.

(20) **Keep your chin up (stay cheerful) :** I was delighted to know that he was keeping his chin up despite all his difficulties. John took it all on the chin, though he was severely criticized by his boss.

(21) **Turn a deaf ear** (refuse to listen to somebody or something) He turned a deaf ear to our warning and thus got into trouble.

(22) **Elbow one's way through** (force one's way by using one's Elbow .The conference room was so crowded that I had to elbow my way through the crowd to reach my seat.

(23) **Not bat an eye/eyelash/eyelid** (not show any shock or surprise) So what did she say when you told her you were leaving?' 'She didn't bat an eyelid.'

(24) **Turn a blind eye** (choose to ignore behavior that you know is wrong) I knew Peter was taking the money but I turned a blind eye because he was my nephew.

(25) Keep an eye on (keep a watch on)

I decided to keep an eye on him because I found his way of working suspicious.

(26) In the eyes of somebody (in somebody's judgment)

In my eyes he is a good and honest man.

(27) Doesn't see eye to eye (If two people don't see eye to eye, they don't agree with each other.) He's asked for a transfer because he doesn't see eye to eye with the new manager .

(28) Face up to (meet or accept challenges boldly)

I never thought that he would be able to face up to the difficult situation.

(29) In the face of (in spite of)

He could achieve his goal in the face of great difficulties.

(30) Lose face (do something that may affect your reputation)

He refused to admit his involvement in the scandal because he didn't want to lose face.

(31) Face the music (accept criticism or punishment for something that you have done)

e.g. When it was discovered that he was the culprit, he chose to disappear rather than face the music.

(32) Get cold feet (suddenly become too frightened to do something.

E.g. They were to get married last Sunday, but unfortunately John got cold feet at the last moment.

(33) **Drag your feet/heels** (act in a slow and hesitant manner)

E.g. Peter wants to purchase a new car, but his father is dragging his feet.

(34) **Keep your/both feet on the ground** (not have your character spoilt by becoming famous or successful)

E.g. Success hasn't changed him – he has kept his feet firmly on the ground.

(35) **Stand on one's own feet** (become independent)

E.g. She has finally got a good job – she can now stand on her own feet.

(36) **Not let the grass grow under your feet** (not waste time by delaying doing something)

E.g. Students, your exams are fast approaching – you can hardly afford to let the grass grow under your feet.

(37) **Have the world at your feet** (become extremely successful and popular) Her first film has just released, but the young actress already has the world at her feet.

(38) **Get something across** - cause people to understand or accept it

E.g. Though he tried hard, he couldn't get the new idea across.

E.g. He could get the message across without much difficulty.

(39) **Get after - pursue;** attack

E.g. Though they got after the thieves, the policemen failed to arrest them.

(40) **Get along** - live sociably with somebody; manage; make progress

E.g. I don't understand how he manages to get along with her.

(41) **Get at** - reach; find out

E.g. Though he tried hard, the hungry fox couldn't get at the bunch of grapes. **E.g**. They are trying to get at the truth.

(42) **Get away (with)** - leave; escape; avoid the penalty of

E.g. The rich lad probably believed that he would be able to get away with the murder, but he was proved wrong.

(43) **Get off** – start : We got off in the morning.

Get off - escape punishment : The accused couldn't get off.

(44) **Get over** –overcome : He could get over the financial difficulties easily.

(45) **Get round somebody** - persuade somebody to do what is desired; outwit; influence: A pretty young wife easily gets round an old husband.

(46) **Break down** – fail to work, go wrong; prove to be wrong.

The machine broke down.

Break down – be overcome by emotion: She broke down in the middle of her speech.

(47) **Break into** – get into by force: The police broke into the building to capture the thieves.

(48) **Break in** – train someone: We need a trainer to break our pony in.

(49) **Break off** – stop abruptly, as in talking

He broke off in the middle of his speech.

(50) **Break out** – appear suddenly

Plague has broken out in the city.

(51) Break up – (of a meeting, school term etc.) end

The meeting broke up at 10 pm.

Break up – disperse: The police used tear gas to **break up** the mob.

(52) **Heads will roll**: Something that you say which means people will lose their jobs as punishment for making serious mistakes.

e.g If the accident was caused by company negligence, then heads will roll.

(53) **head to toe**: She was tall and thin and dressed head to toe in black He was washed from head to toe

(53) **Head over heels**: Often used with fall to describe the beginning of a relationship e.g They met at a night club and instantly fell head over heels for one another

(54) **A game of two halves** : Circumstances have changed suddenly; E;g

(55) **In abeyance :** not operating, E.g. The title shall be deemed to be in abeyance.

(56) **Abide by** : to accept, E. g. Germany and Russia agreed informally to abide by the agreement.

(57) **To keep abreast of :** to know the most recent facts : E.g. They were of course well abreast of the war situation.

(58) **To give a good account of :** behave in a way which brings you praise: E.g. Your son gave a very good account of himself.

(59) **Achilles heel: weakest point:** E.g. Rude behavior is businessman's Achilles heel.

(60) **Ad infinitum:** repeated again and again : E.g. She teaches virtues to her daughter ad infinitum.

(61) **Ad nauseam :** to do something repeatedly over a long period of time: E.g. She went on ad nauseam about how well her children were doing at school.

(62) **Across the board**: including everyone or everything ; The computer company decided to give the workers an across –the –board increase in their salary

(63) **Hanky panky** ; double dealing . Trickery , cheating

(64) **Hard and fast** : rigidly adhered to :

(65) **Hit the nail on the head**: Do or say something exactly right and precise.

(66) **Hobson's choice:** no choice at all :

(67) **I ''ll wear my heart upon my sleeve** : Display your feeling openly.

(68) **In someone's bad book:** to be in disgrace or out of favor.

(69) **Keep body and soul together** : to survive , earn sufficient money to keep oneself alive

(70) **Bail a company out**: help or rescue a company with financial problems

E.g The government decided to bail out the failing bank in order to maintain stability in the economy.

(71) **Bottom line** : the total , the final figure on the balance sheet

e.g When they examined the bottom line of the company they decided not to invest in it .

(72) **Budget squeeze** / crunch : a situation where there is not enough money in th Budget E.g We have been going through a severe budget squeeze at our company and must begin to stop spending money in a wasteful manner.

(73) **Buy off** : use a gift or money to divert someone from their duty or purpose

E.g the land developer tried to buy off the politicians but he was not successful.

(74) **Buy out** : Buy the ownership or a decisive share of something

E. g The company was bought out by another large company in textile industry.

(75) **By a long shot** : By a big difference : the soap company was able to beat out the bids of other companies by a long shot.

(76) **Clcaulated risk:** An action that may fail but has a good chance to succeed. e.g They took a calculated risk when they introduced the new computer screen onto the market.

(77) **Carry over:** save for another time : We were forced to carry over the sale to Monday after the national holiday. E.g Our company is still facing difficult time and we will have to carry over last year's losses to this year.

(78) **Carry the day** : win completely , E.g the president's new idea carried the day and every one supported him energetically

(79) **Carry through** : put into action, E.g the steel company carried through their plan to restructure all of their operations

(80) **Close out** : sell the whole of something , e. g they decided to close out the store and sell all of the remaining stock very cheap

(81) **Cold call** : Call a potential customer from a list of persons one has never seen e.g When he first started to work at his company he was asked to make cold calls using the telephone book .

(82) **Come on strong** : overwhelm with excessively strong language or personality, E.g the salesman came on too strong at the meeting and angered the other members of the team.

(83) **Change hands** : to be moved from one owner to another : E.g The hotel has changed hands twice since 1982.

(84) **Change off:** to alternate in doing something . E.g Tom and I changed off so neither of us had to answer the phone all the time,.

(85) **Build castle in the air**: to daydream. E,g To make plan that can never come true.

(86) **company man** : a person who always works hard and agrees with his employees e.g My father was a true company man and always putting in an extra effort for his company

(87) **Deliver goods** : Succeed in doing well what is expected: e.g The new owner of the company is not very popular but he is able to deliver the goods.

(88) **Double Check** : Check something again to confirm: e.g we were unable to double Check the costs of the new products before the price list was printed.

(89) **The official worth or trust of something :** e.g although the face value of the postage stamp was very low it sold at the auction for much money.

(90) **Fair play :** justice , equal and right action to someone .

E. g you should use fair play while bargaining with their employees.

(91) **Finger in the pie:** Involved in what is happening, receiving money for something. e.g The new manager has his finger in the pie in all aspects of company's business.

(92) **gain ground** : go forward : E.g Our company has been gaining ground in our attempt to be the best in the industry.

(93) **All's well that ends well** Meaning : We have few concerns if things turn out

(94) **Keep the ball rolling** :Maintain a level of activity in and enthusiasm for a project

(95) **lame duck** : a person isn't able to function, especially one that was previously proficient.

4.3 IMPORTANT SAYINGS AND QUOTATIONS

(1) Beauty is truth, truth beauty, —that is all Ye know on earth, and all ye need to know. **John Keats**

(2) What the imagination seizes as beauty must be the truth. **John Keats**

(3) I never teach my pupils. I only attempt to provide the conditions in which they can learn. **Albert Einstein**

(4) Try not to become a man of success but rather to become a man of value **Albert Einstein**

(5) The true teacher defends his pupils against his own personal influence. **Amos Bronson Alcott**

(6) The whole art of teaching is only the art of awakening the natural curiosity of young minds for the purpose of satisfying it afterwards. **Anatole France**

(7) Teachers open the door. You enter by yourself. **Chinese proverb**

(8) From error to error one discovers the entire truth. **Sigmund Freud**

(9) The more the fruits of knowledge become accessible to men, the more widespread is the decline of religious belief. **Sigmund Freud**

(10) A man's silence is wonderful to listen to. **Thomas Hardy**

(11) Tis better to be silent and be thought a fool, than to speak and remove all doubt. **Abraham Lincoln**

(12) He who does not know how to be silent will not know how to speak. **Ausonius**

(13) Silence is the most perfect expression of scorn. **George Bernard Shaw**

(14) The most profound statements are often said in silence. **Lynn Johnston**

(15) Well-timed silence hath more eloquence than speech. **Martin Farquhar Tupper**

(16) Silence is golden when you can't think of a good answer. **Mohammad Ali**

(17) If winter comes, can spring be far behind? **Percy Bysshe shelley**

(18) Poetry is the record of the best and happiest moments of the happiest and best minds. **Percy Bysshe shelley**

(19) True genius is always inborn and never cultivated, let alone learned. Adolf Hitler

(20) Man is so mad that he can only find relaxation from one kind of labor by taking up another (**Antole France**)

(21) Real success is finding your life work in the work that you love.**(David Mc Cullough)**

(22) All human being must have occupation if he or she is not to become a nuisance to the world. (**Dorothy L. Sayers)**

(23) Get happiness out of your work or you may never know what happiness is. **(Elbert Hubbard)**

(24) Measure not the work until the day's out and the labor done. (**Barret Browning)**

(25) Do not hire a man who does your work for money but him who does it for love of it . (**Henry David Thoreau)**

(26) When tour work speaks for itself, don't interrupt. **(Henry J. Kaiser)**

(27) People forget how fast you did a job –but they remember how well you did it. (Howard Newton)

(28) The sweat of hard work is not to be displayed. It is much more graceful to appeared favored by the gods. **(Maxine Hong Kingstone)**

(29) People who work sitting down get paid more than people who work standing Up. (**Ogden Nash)**

(30) Age can't wither her , nor custom stale her infinite variety : **(Shakespeare' s** Antony and Cleopatra 1606)

(31) Life is like a play, we merely go through the stages of our life acting it out **(As You Like It) Shakespeare**

(32) All's well that ends well (1602) Meaning: We have few concerns if things turn out Well in the end.(**Shakespeare)**

(33) Brevity is the soul of wit : **Hamlet 1603 (Shakespeare)**

(34) Discretion is the better part of valour **(Shakespeare)**

(35) How sharper than a serpent' tooth it is to have thankless child. **(Shakespeare)**

(36) A bird in the hand is worth two in the bush. Meaning : It's better to have a small advantage than the chance of a greater one. **18th Century** . taken from from a song entitled **(A Bird in the Hand is Worth Two in the Bush)**

(37) Better one bird in hand than ten in the wood

(38) A Fool's Paradise : A state of happiness based on false hope. Romeo and Juliet **(Shakespeare)**

(39) A countenance more in sorrow than in anger : a person that is viewed more with sadness than with anger (Hamlet 1607) **Shakespeare**

(40) A rose by any other name would smell as sweet. Meaning: What matters is if something is not what it is called. (Romeo and Juliet 1594)

(41) Genius is one percent inspiration and 99 percent perspiration. Meaning: A saying that extols the benefits of hard works and effort. **(Thomas Alva Edison)**

(42) If music be the food of love play on **.(Shakespeare)**

(43) It's better to light a candle than curse the darkness. **By John Kennedy**

(44) It is better to give than to receive. **Bible**:

(45) **Let a thousand flowers bloom :** Encourage many ideas from many Sources: Chinese proverb :

(46) **Make a virtue of necessity: Chaucer's saying** . one is willing doing something in fact he couldn't avoid doing

(47) **Man doesn't live by bread alone :** Physical nourishment is not sufficient for a healthy life , man also has spiritual needs

(48) **Many a little makes a mickle:** Many small amounts accumulate to make a large amount. Mickle or as muckle meaning a large size in Scotland

(49) A little knowledge is a dangerous thing

(50) A miss is as good as a mile

(51) A stitch in time saves nine :

(52) A volunteer is worth twenty pressed men

(53) Absolute power corrupts absolutely

(54) All that glitters is not gold : A showy article may not necessarily be valuable

(55) All's fair in love and war

(56) As you sow so shall you reap

(57) Attack is the best form of defence

(58) Barking dogs seldom bite

(59) Beauty is in the eye of beholder

(60) Beauty is only skin deep

(61) hind every great man there is a great woman.

(62) Better late than never

(63) Cleanliness is next to godliness

(64) Don't bite the hands that feed you

(65) Don't change horses in midstream :Don't change your leader in mids by **Abraham Lincoln**

(66) Easy come, easy go

(67) Enough is enough

(68) Every body wants to go to heaven but nobody wants to die.

(69) Fools rush where angels fear to tread

(70) Forewarned is forearmed

(71) Fortunes favor the brave

(72) Good fences make good neighbors

(73) Meet your waterloo: arrive at a final decisive contest:

(74) Milk of human kindness: Care and compassion for others

(75) Much ado about nothing: A great deal of fuss over nothing of importance

(76) Mumbo Jumbo: Nonsense, especially meaningless speech and often associated with spurious religious rituals

(77) Murphy's law: Whatever can go wrong will go wrong

(78) My better half: My husband or my wife: by Roman poet Horace.

(79) salad days : The days of one's youthful experience

(80) Nitty –gritty: The heart of the matter, the basic essentials, the harsh realities

(81) Nothing succeeds like success: success breeds further success

(82) Off the record: Something said in confidence

(83) Paddle you own canoe: Decide your own fate;

(84) A pen is mightier than the sword

(85) Rack your brains : to strain mentally to recall or to understand something

Many verbs in English are followed by an adverb or a preposition (also called a particle) and these two part verbs also called phrasal verbs are different from verbs with helpers. The particle that follows the verbs changes the meaning of the phrasal verbs in idiomatic ways :

(1) **drop off: decline gradually** : The hill dropped off near the river

(2) **drop off: fall asleep**: While doing his homework , he dropped off

(3) **Drop off: Stop and give something to someone** ; Would you drop this off at the post office.

(4) **Drop out : cease to participate**: After two laps, the runner dropped out

Some particles can be separated from the verb so that a noun and pronoun can be inserted and some particles can't be separated from the verb. In addition, some phrases are intransitive meaning they cann't take a direct object

Separable: add up

(1) she added up the total on her calculator

(2) She added it up on her calculator Both bare correct

Inseparable : get around

(1) Correct : She always gets around the rules.

(2) Incorrect : She always gets the rules around (makes no sense in English)

Intransitive : Catch on (meaning to understand)

Correct : After I explained the math problem she began to catch on .

Incorrect : She began to catch on the math problem . (catch on can't take a direct object in this meaning)

Correct : She began to catch on to the math problem

4.4. USAGE

(1) **Abstruse-Obtuse: Obtuse** dull, stupid." But people often mix the word up with "**abstruse,"** which means "difficult to understand. When you mean to criticize something for being needlessly complex or baffling, the word you need is not "obtuse," but "abstruse."

(2) **Accede-Exceed**: If you drive too fast, you exceed the speed limit. "Accede" is a much rarer word meaning "give in," "agree."

(3) **Advance – Advanced**: When you hear about something in advance, earlier than other people, you get advance notice or information. "Advanced" means "complex, sophisticated" and doesn't necessarily have anything to do with the revealing of secrets.

(4) **Adverse- Averse**: The word "adverse" turns up most frequently in the phrase "adverse circumstances," meaning difficult circumstances, circumstances which act as an *adversary;* but people often confuse this word with "averse," a much rarer word, meaning having a strong feeling against, or *aversion* toward.

(5) **Aesthetic – Ascetic**: "Aesthetic" (also spelled "esthetic") has to do with beauty, whereas "ascetic" has to do with avoiding pleasure, including presumably the pleasure of looking at beautiful things. St. Francis had an ascetic attitude toward life, whereas Oscar Wilde had an esthetic attitude toward life.

(6) **Afterwards- Afterwords**: Like "towards," "forwards," and "homewards,". "afterwards" ends with *-wards*. "Afterwords" are sometimes the explanatory essays at the ends of books or speeches uttered at the end of plays or other works. They are made up of *words*.

(7) **Alliterate- illiterate ;** Pairs of words which begin with the same sound are said to alliterate, like "wild and wooly." Those who can't read are illiterate.

(8) **Allude- Elude**: You can allude (refer) to your daughter's membership in the honor of the society when boasting about her, but a criminal tries to elude (escape) captivity. There no such word as "illude.

(9) **Allusion- Illusion** : An allusion is a reference, something you *allude* to: "Her allusion to flowers reminded me that Valentine's Day was coming." In that English paper, don't write "literary illusions" when you mean "allusions." A mirage, hallucination, or a magic trick is an *illusion*. (Doesn't being fooled just make you *ill?*)

(10) **Allusive/ Elusive/ Illusive** : When a lawyer alludes to his client's poor mother, he is being *allusive*. When the mole keeps eluding the traps you've set in the garden, it's being *elusive*. We also speak of matters that are difficult to understand, identify, or remember as elusive. Illusions can be *illusive*, but we more often refer to them as *illusory*.

(11) **All ready/ Already:** "All ready" is a phrase meaning "completely prepared," as in "As soon as I put my coat

on, I'll be all ready." "Already," however, is an adverb used to describe something that has happened before a certain time, as in "What do you mean you'd rather stay home? I've already got my coat on."

(12) **Alternate/ Alternative**: Although UK authorities disapprove, in U.S. usage, "alternate" is frequently an adjective, substituted for the older "alternative": "an alternate route." "Alternate" can also be a noun; a substitute delegate is, for instance, called an "alternate." But when you're speaking of "every other" as in "our club meets on alternate Tuesdays," you can't substitute "alternative."

(13) **Altogether/ All together** : Altogether" is an adverb meaning "completely," "entirely." For example: "When he first saw the examination questions, he was altogether baffled." "All together," in contrast, is a phrase meaning "in a group." For example: "The wedding guests were gathered all together in the garden." Undressed people are said in informal speech to be "in the altogether" (perhaps a shortening of the phrase "altogether naked").

(14) **Amongst/ among:** Although "amongst" has not dated nearly as badly as "whilst," it is still less common in standard speech than "among."

(15) **Amoral/ Immoral**: "Amoral" is a rather technical word meaning "unrelated to morality." When you mean to denounce someone's behavior, call it "immoral."

(16) **Altar/ Alter;** An *altar* is that platform at the front of a church or in a temple; to *alter* something is to change it.

(17) **Anecdotes/ Antidotes:** A humorist relates "anecdotes." The doctor prescribes "antidotes" for children who have swallowed poison. Laughter may be the best medicine, but that's no reason to confuse these two with each other.

(18) **Appraise/ Apprise:** When you estimate the value of something, you *appraise* it. When you inform people of a situation, you *apprise* them of it.

(19) **Backwards/ Backward :** As an adverb, either word will do: "put the shirt on backward" or "put the shirt on backwards." However, as an adjective, only "backward" will do: "a backward glance." When in doubt, use "backward."

(20) **Benefactors/ Beneficiary**: Benefactors give benefits; beneficiaries receive them. We expect to hear of generous benefactors and grateful beneficiaries.

(21) **Breathe/ Breath**: When you need to breathe, you take a breath. "Breathe" is the verb, "breath" the noun.

(22) **By/ Bye/ Buy:** These are probably confused with each other more often through haste than through actual ignorance, but "by" is the common preposition in phrases like "you should know by now." It can also serve a number of other functions, but the main point here is not to confuse "by" with the other two spellings: "'bye" is an abbreviated form of "goodbye" (preferably with an apostrophe before it to indicate the missing syllable), and "buy" is the verb meaning "purchase." "Buy" can also be a noun, as in "that was a great buy." The term for the position of a competitor who advances to the next level of a tournament without playing is a "bye." All others are "by."

(23) **Cannot/ Can not:** These two spellings are largely interchangeable, but by far the most common is "cannot" and you should probably use it except when you want to be emphatic: "No, you can *not* wash the dog in the Maytag."

(24) **Cannon/ Canon :** "Canon" used to be such a rare word that there was no temptation to confuse it with "cannon": a large piece of artillery. The debate over the

literary canon (a list of officially-approved works) and the popularity of Pachelbel's Canon (an imitative musical form related to the common "round") have changed all that—confusion is rampant. Just remember that the big gun is a "cannon." All the rest are "canons." Note that there are metaphorical uses of "cannon" for objects shaped like large guns, such as a horse's "cannon bone."

(25) **Carrot/ carats/ Karat/ caret :** Carrots" are those crunchy orange vegetables Bugs Bunny is so fond of, but this spelling gets misused for the less familiar words which are pronounced the same but have very different meanings. Precious stones like diamonds are weighed in *carats*. The same word is used to express the proportion of pure gold in an alloy, though in this usage it is sometimes spelled "karat" (hence the abbreviation "20K gold"). A *caret* is a proofreader's mark showing where something needs to be inserted, shaped like a tiny pitched roof. It looks rather like a French circumflex, but is usually distinct from it on modern computer keyboards. Carets are extensively used in computer programming. Just remember, if you can't eat it, it's not a *carrot*.

(26) **Censor/ censure/ sensor/censer:** To *censor* somebody's speech or writing is to try to suppress it by preventing it from reaching the public. When guests on network TV utter obscenities, broadcasters practice censorship by bleeping them.

To *censure* someone, however, is to officially denounce an offender. You can be censured as much for actions as for words. A lawyer who destroyed evidence which would have been unfavorable to his client might be censured by the bar association.

A device which senses any change like changes in light or electrical output is a *sensor*. Your car and your digital camera contain sensors. A *censer* is a church incense burner.

(27) **Cite/ Site/ Sight;** You *cite* the author in an end note; you visit a Web *site* or the *site* of the crime, and you *sight* your beloved running toward you in slow motion on the beach (a sight for sore eyes!).

(28) **Coarse/ Course: Coarse**" is always an adjective meaning "rough, crude." Unfortunately, this spelling is often mistakenly used for a quite different word, "course," which can be either a verb or a noun (with several different meanings.

(29) **Collaborate/ Corroborate**: People who work together on a project *collaborate* (share their labor); people who support your testimony as a witness *corroborate* (strengthen by confirming) it.

(30) **Collage/ College:** You can paste together bits of paper to make a collage, but the institution of higher education is a *college.*

(31) **Compliment/ Complement**; Originally these two spellings were used interchangeably, but they have come to be distinguished from each other in modern times. Most of the time the word people intend is "compliment": nice things said about someone ("She paid me the compliment of admiring the way I shined my shoes."). "Complement," much less common, has a number of meanings associated with matching or completing. Complements supplement each other, each adding something the others lack, so we can say that "Alice's love for entertaining and Mike's love for washing dishes complement each other." Remember, if you're not making nice to someone, the word is "complement."

(32) **Complimentary/ complementary**: When paying someone a compliment like "I love what you've done with the kitchen!" you're being complimentary. A free bonus item is also a complimentary gift. But items or people that go well with each other are complementary.

(33) **Continuously/ Continually:** Continuous" refers to actions which are uninterrupted: "My upstairs neighbor played his stereo continuously from 6:00 PM to 3:30 AM." Continual actions, however, need not be uninterrupted, only repeated: "My father continually urges me to get a job."

(34) **Copyright/ Copywrite:** You can copyright writing, but you can also copyright a photograph or song. The word has to do with securing *rights*. Thus, there is no such word as "copywritten"; it's "copyrighted."

(35) **Council/ counsels/ consul;** The first two words are pronounced the same but have distinct meanings. An official group that deliberates, like the *council in foreign Relations,* is a "council"; all the rest are "counsels": your lawyer, advice, etc. A consul is a local representative of a foreign government.

(36) **Defuse/Diffuse** ; You defuse a dangerous situation by treating it like a bomb and removing its fuse; to diffuse, in contrast, is to spread something out: "Bob's cheap cologne diffused throughout the room, wrecking the wine-tasting."

(37) **Denigrate/ downgrade/ degrade** : Many people use "downgrade" instead of "denigrate" to mean "defame, slander." "Downgrade" is entirely different in meaning. When something is downgraded, it is lowered in grade (usually made worse), not just *considered* worse. "When the president of the company fled to Rio with fifteen million dollars, its bonds were *downgraded* to junk bond status." "Degrade" is much more flexible in meaning. It can mean to lower in status or rank (like "downgrade") or to corrupt or make contemptible; but it always has to do with actual reduction in value rather than mere insult, like "denigrate." Most of the time when people use "downgrade" they would be better off instead using "insult," "belittle," or "sneer at."

(38) **Dessert/ Desert:** Perhaps these two words are confused partly because "dessert" is one of the few words in English with a double "S" pronounced like "Z" ("brassiere" is another). That impoverished stretch of sand called a desert can only afford one "S." In contrast, that rich gooey extra thing at the end of the meal called a dessert indulges in two of them. The word in the phrase "he got his just deserts" is confusingly pronounced just like "desserts."

(39) **Disburse/ disperse:** You disburse money by taking it out of your purse (French "bourse") and distributing it. If you refuse to hand out any money, the eager mob of beggars before you may disperse (scatter).

(40) **Discreet/discrete**: The more common word is "discreet," meaning "prudent, circumspect": "When arranging the party for Agnes, be sure to be discreet; we want her to be surprised." "Discrete" means "separate, distinct": "He arranged the guest list into two discrete groups: meat-eaters and vegetarians." Note how the *T* separates the two *Es* in "discrete."

(41) **Download / Upload:** Most people do far more downloading (transferring files to their computers) than uploading (transferring files from their computers), so it's not surprising that they often use the first word for the second word's meaning. You don't download the video of your birthday party but you upload it.

(42) **Eminent/ imminent/ Immanent** By far the most common of these words is "eminent," meaning "prominent, famous." "Imminent," in phrases like "facing imminent disaster," means "threatening." It comes from Latin *minere*, meaning "to project or overhang." Think of a mine threatening to cave in. Positive events can also be imminent: they just need to be coming soon. The rarest of the three is "immanent," used by philosophers to mean "inherent" and by theologians to mean

"present throughout the universe" when referring to God. It comes from Latin *manere*, "remain." Think of God creating man in his own image.

(43) **Emigrate:** to leave one's old country. **Immigrate** is to enter a new country. **Migrate** is to travel from country to country, usually on a regular basis, and nowadays more often refers to birds and African antelopes than people— with the exception of 'migrant workers'.

It needn't be the speaker's country. *Japanese **emigrated** from Japan and **immigrated** to Brazil. Germans **emigrated** from Germany and **immigrated** to Mexico. The Jews **emigrated** from Pharaonic Egypt and **immigrated** to the Promised Land.*

(44) **Egoist (also Egotist)**: a person who is selfish, self absorbed and self centered.

(45) **Imitate/ emulate:** People generally know what "imitate" means, but they sometimes don't understand that "emulate" is a more specialized word with a purely positive function, meaning to try to equal or match. Thus if you try to climb the same mountain your big brother did, you're emulating him; but if you copy his habit of sticking peas up his nose, you're just imitating him.

(46) **Forego/ Forgo :** The E in "forego" tells you it has to do with going *before.* It occurs mainly in the expression "foregone conclusion," a conclusion arrived at in advance. "Forgo" means to abstain from or do without. "After finishing his steak, he decided to *forgo* the blueberry cheesecake."

(47) **foresee / foresee**: This word means "to see into the future." There are lots of words with the prefix "fore-" which are future-oriented, including "foresight," "foretell," "forethought," and "foreword," all of which are often misspelled by people who omit the *E.* Just

remember: what golfers shout when they are warning people ahead of them about the shot they are about to make is *"fore*

(48) **forwards/ Forward:** Although some style books prefer "forward" and "toward" to "forwards" and "towards," none of these forms is really incorrect, though the forms without the final S are perhaps a smidgen more formal. The same generally applies to "backward" and "backwards." There are a few expressions in which only one of the two forms works: step forward, forward motion, a backward child. The spelling "foreword" applies exclusively to the introductory matter in a book

(49) **Gray/ grey:** Gray" is the American spelling, "grey" the British spelling of this color/colour. When it's part of a British name—like Tarzan's title, "Lord Greystoke"—or part of a place name—like "Greyfriars"—it should retain its original spelling even if an American is doing the writing.

(50) **Handicap/ disable;** In normal usage, a handicap is a drawback you can easily remedy, but a disability is much worse: you're just unable to do something. But many people with disabilities and those who work with them strongly prefer "disability" to "handicap," which they consider an insulting term. Their argument is that a disability can be compensated for by—for instance—a wheelchair, so that the disabled person is not handicapped. Only the person truly unable by any means to accomplish tasks because of a disability is handicapped. The fact that this goes directly counter to ordinary English usage may help to explain why the general public has been slow to adopt it; but if you want to avoid offending anyone, you're safer using "disability" than "handicap."

Many of the people involved also resent being called "disabled people"; they prefer "people with disabilities

(51) **Hangar/ Hanger:** You park your plane in a hangar but hang up your slackon is a hanger.

(21) ***Heal / Heel:*** *Heal* is what you do when you get better. Your *heel* is the back part of your foot. Achilles' heel was the only place the great warrior could be wounded in such a way that the injury wouldn't heal. Thus any striking weakness can be called an "Achilles' heel." To remember the meaning of "heal," note that it is the beginning of the word "health."

(53) **historic/ Historical:** The meaning of "historic" has been narrowed down to "famous in history." One should not call a building, site, district, or event "historical." Sites may be of historical interest if historians are interested in them, but not just because they are old. In America "historic" is grossly overused as a synonym for "older than my father's day."

(54) **Infamous/ Notorious**: Infamous" means famous in a bad way. It is related to the word "infamy." Humorists have for a couple of centuries jokingly used the word in a positive sense, but the effectiveness of the joke depends on the listener knowing that this is a misuse of the term. Because this is a very old joke indeed you should stick to using "infamous" only of people like Hitler and Billy the Kid. Notorious means the same thing as "infamous" and should also only be used in a negative sense.

(55) **Intense/ Intensive**: If you are putting forth an intense effort, your work is "intense": "My intense study of Plato convinced me that I would make a good leader." But when the intensity stems not so much from your effort as it does from outside forces, the usual word is "intensive": "the village endured intensive bombing."

(56) **Minor/ miner:** Children are minors, but unless they are violating child-labor laws, those who work in mines are *miners*.

(57) **Moral/ Morale:** If you are trying to make people behave properly, you are policing their morals; if you are just trying to keep their spirits up, you are trying to maintain their morale. "Moral" is accented on the first syllable, "morale" on the second.

(58) **Oppress/ repress:** Dictators commonly oppress their citizens and repress dissent, but these words don't mean exactly the same thing. "Repress" just means "keep under control." sometimes repression is a good thing: "During the job interview, repress the temptation to tell Mr. Brown that he has toilet paper stuck to his shoe." Oppression is always bad, and implies serious persecution

(59) **Verbal/ Oral:** Some people insist that "verbal" refers to anything expressed in words, whether written or spoken, while "oral" refers exclusively to speech; but in common usage "verbal" has become widely accepted for the latter meaning. However, in legal contexts, an unwritten agreement is still an "oral contract," not a "verbal contract

(60) **Loath/ Loathe:** Loath" is a rather formal adjective meaning reluctant and rhymes with "both," whereas "loathe" is a common verb meaning to dislike intensely, and rhymes with "clothe." Kenji is loath to go to the conference at Kilauea because he loathes volcanos.

(61) **Oversee/ overlook :** When you oversee the preparation of dinner, you take control and manage the operation closely. But if you overlook the preparation of dinner you forget to prepare the meal entirely—better order pizza.

(62) **Overtake/ Take over:** When you catch up with the runners ahead of you in a marathon, you overtake them; but when you seize power, you take over the government.

(63) **Perpetrate/ perpetuate;** Perpetrate" is something criminals do (criminals are sometimes called "perps" in cop slang). When you seek to continue something you are trying to perpetuate it.

(64) **Persecute/ prosecute:** When you persecute someone, you're treating them badly, whether they deserve it or not; but only legal officers can prosecute someone for a crime.

(65) **Perspective/ prospective:** Perspective" has to do with sight, as in painting, and is usually a noun. "Prospective" generally has to do with the future (compare with "What are your prospects, young man?") and is usually an adjective. But beware: there is also a rather old-fashioned but fairly common meaning of the word "prospect" that has to do with sight: "as he climbed the mountain, a vast prospect opened up before him."

(66) **populace/ populous:** The population of a country may be referred to as its populace, but a crowded country is populous.

(67) **Prophecy/ Prophesy** : Prophecy," the noun, (pronounced "PROF-a-see") is a prediction. The verb "to prophesy" (pronounced "PROF-a-sigh") means to predict something. When a prophet prophesies he or she utters prophecies.

Outside of Bob Dylan's lyrics, writers and critics do not "prophesize." They prophesy.

(68) **Purposely/ Purposefully:** If you do something on purpose (not by accident), you do it purposely. But if you have a specific purpose in mind, you are acting purposefully.

(69) **Rational/ Rationale:** Rational" is an adjective meaning "reasonable" or "logical": "I have made a rational

decision to sell his old car when he moved to New York." "Rational" rhymes with "national."

"Rationale" is a noun which most often means "underlying reason": "His rationale for this decision was that it would cost more to pay for parking than the car was worth." "Rationale" rhymes with "passion pal."

(70) Ravage/ Ravish/Ravenous: To ravage is to pillage, sack, or devastate. The only time "ravaging" is properly used is in phrases like "when the pirates had finished ravaging the town, they turned to ravishing the women." Which brings us to "ravish": meaning to rape, or rob violently. A trailer court can be ravaged by a storm (nothing is stolen, but a lot of damage is done) but not ravished. The crown jewels of Ruritania can be ravished (stolen using violence) without being ravaged (damaged).

To confuse matters, people began back in the fourteenth century to speak metaphorically of their souls being "ravished" by intense spiritual or esthetic experiences. Thus we speak of a "ravishing woman" (the term is rarely applied to men) today not because she literally rapes men who look at her but because her devastating beauty penetrates their hearts in an almost violent fashion. Despite contemporary society's heightened sensitivity about rape, we still remain (perhaps fortunately) unconscious of many of the transformations of the root meaning in words with positive connotations such as "rapturous."

Originally, "raven" as a verb was synonymous with "ravish" in the sense of "to steal by force." One of its specialized meanings became "devour," as in "the lion ravened her prey." By analogy, hungry people became "ravenous" (as hungry as beasts), and that remains the only common use of the word today.

If a woman smashes your apartment up, she ravages it. If she looks stunningly beautiful, she is ravishing. If she eats the whole platter of hors d'oeuvres you've set out for the party before the other guests come, she's ravenous.

(71) **Restrain/ Refrain :** Restrain" is a transitive verb: it needs an object. Although "refrain" was once a synonym for "restrain" it is now an intransitive verb: it should not have an object. Here are examples of correct modern usage: "When I pass the doughnut shop I have to restrain myself" ("myself" is the object). "When I feel like throwing something at my boss, I usually refrain from doing so." You can't *refrain* yourself or anyone else.

(72) **remuneration/ Renumeration**: Although "remuneration" looks as if it might mean "repayment" it usually means simply "payment." In speech it is often confused with When something is standing still, it's *stationary.* That piece of paper you write a letter on is *stationery.* Let the "E" in "stationery" remind you of "envelope." "renumeration," which would mean re-counting (counting again).

(73) **Stationary/ stationery**: When something is standing still, it's *stationary:* That piece of paper you write a letter on is *stationery.* Let the "E" in "stationery" remind you of "envelope."

(74) **Timber/ Timbre :** You can build a house out of timber, but that quality which distinguishes the sound produced by one instrument or voice from others is *timbre*, usually pronounced "TAM-bruh," so the common expression is "vocal timbre."

(75) **Undo/ Undue :** The verb "undo" is the opposite of "do." You undo your typing errors on a computer or undo your shoelaces to go wading.

The adjective "undue" is the opposite of "due" and means "unwarranted" or "improper." It is used in phrases like "undue influence," "undue burdens," and "undue expense."

(76) **Vain/ vane / Vein :** When you have vanity you are conceited: you are vain. "You're so vain you probably think this song is about you." This spelling can also mean "futile," as in "All my love's in vain" (fruitless). Note that when Ecclesiastes says that "all is vanity" it doesn't mean that everything is conceited, but that everything is pointless.

A vane is a blade designed to move or be moved by gases or liquid, like a weathervane.

A vein is a slender thread of something, like blood in a body or gold in a mine. It can also be a line of thought, as in "After describing his dog's habit of chewing on the sofa, Carlos went on in the same vein for several minutes.

(77) **Vicious Circle/** The term "vicious circle" was invented by logicians to describe a form of fallacious circular argument in which each term of the argument draws on the other: "Democracy is the best form of government because democratic elections produce the best governments." The phrase has been extended in popular usage to all kinds of self-exacerbating processes such as this: poor people often find themselves borrowing money to pay off their debts, but in the process create even more onerous debts which in their turn will need to be financed by further borrowing. Sensing vaguely that such destructive spirals are not closed loops, people have transmuted "vicious circle" into "vicious cycle." The problem with this perfectly logical change is that a lot of people know what the original "correct" phrase was and are likely to scorn users of the new one. They go beyond

scorn to contempt however toward those poor souls who render the phrase as "viscous cycle." Don't use this expression unless you are discussing a Harley-Davidson in dire need of an oil change

(78) **Wet your appetite :** It is natural to think that something mouth-watering "wets your appetite," but actually the expression is "whet your appetite"— sharpen your appetite, as a whetstone sharpens a knife.

(79) ***Wide, broad*** *refer to dimensions. They are often interchangeable, but* ***wide*** *especially applies to things of which the length is much greater than the width: a wide road, piece of ribbon.* ***Broad*** *is more emphatic, and applies to things of considerable or great width, breadth, or extent, esp. to surfaces extending laterally: a broad valley.* (Random House Dict)

REFERECES

(1) Norman Lewis (1994) Word Power Made Easy, General Book Depot, Naisarak, Delhi.

(2) Collins Cobuild English Language Dictionary

CHAPTER-5

WRITING AND READING SKILLS WITH MEDIA TECHNOLOGY

5.1.1 Writing Skill: Of all the four categories of language skills writing is by far the most difficult for native as well as non-native users of English language. The enormous field of literary criticism reveals the fact that one tends to judge writing skill far more critically than any other language activity. This critical finding of creativity doesn't confine itself to literature, but it covers the wide range , such as the school of journalism, letter writing, correspondence, and the art of the concise memorandam. All indicate that good writing is an elite occupation and it requires subsequent practice. But it is rather surprising that no considerable attention has yet been paid to writing skill and no systematic practice has been taught to students in college and in universities consequently in this area the major section of learners is lagging behind. This unit deals with some important issues regarding the various aspect of writing at advanced levels and how television / video can be exploited to improve them considerably.

The recent finding by composition researchers and teachers is concerned with cognitive activity, the primary purpose of which is to generate ideas about a subject. Moreover it gives an important insight into composing process. This research has revealed that composing is a" non-linear exploring and generative process where by writers discover and formulate their ideas and thoughts" **Carroll**[1]. With a view to developing ideas on a particular topic, the process of brainstorming has been found most useful. The primary aim of brain storming is to develop ideas and to acquaint the learners with various aspects of the topic chosen for writing. This device of brainstorming can be satisfactorily accomplished by listening to a group of experts on television and video who are involved in discussing certain topics and issues. Because such a group of elites comes out with novel ideas and thus contribute a lot to the knowledge of the learners leading to the clarity of ideas which is considered as prerequisite for clear and smooth writing . Keeping this in view some cassettes concerning national and international issues should be prepared to facilitate writing tasks of the learners, because intensive ideas on any topic are indispensable for writing at advanced level. Thus television and video can be a great help in widening the learners' ideas. Apart from that , as already stated , that television and video embody a large number of other elements such as visual elements and paralinguistic features which lead to the full comprehension of the topic. Hence description of geological formations, features of weather distillation of comparative temperature charts, historical accounts, brief biographies, all these things can be presented clearly and interestingly on television which are particularly useful for enhancing contemplative, imaginative and visualizing powers.

According to Corbett[2] the words and the phrases associated with visual elements on television / video develop coherence between thought and expression which is usually considered as one of the most important aspects of composition. The composition is generally appreciated only when the writer has maintained the coherence between ideas and expressions. This requires's the writer's ability to recall and visualize the words and phrases which are in tune with the situation. If visual elements are applied through television and video the aspect of appropriateness in composition is most likely to incompass enormously.

By exploiting video materials in the classroom, writing skill of the students can be enhanced considerably . after the students have seen the television or video materials they should be asked to work on the chosen topic. Mutual discussion on the related topic will certainly stimulate the students in generating and organizing ideas.. At this time the students are asked to write and then to exchange compositions so that could deeply analyze each other's works. This is an important aspect of writing experience because it is by responding as readers that students will develop an awareness of the fact that a writing is producing something to be read by someone else.

There are some other devices to develop writing skill at secondary level with the help of television and video. Questions with jumbled answers and clue letter are very helpful to build up vocabulary which facilitate writing a great deal. After showing a short sequence the teacher asked questions on the sentences or characters and gives the answers in jumbled words and give the answers in jumbled words or some clue letters. The learners ase asked to write the correct answers , with the help of the clues provided.

5.1.2 To develop the skill for written communication is very important but it has always been neglected in the academic curriculum. Teachers give no systematic practice for writing to students in the class where as tremendous success in the exam as well as in popularizing research findings worldwide depend mostly on the fair command in written communication, but both the teachers and the students lack motivation for writing skill. On the one hand teachers are less trained to monitor tactfully the students' writing assignment in the class and on the other hand the students also find writing practice so strenuous that they become regularly irregular in the class when they are given writing practice. As a result of this a large number of students remain inefficient in written communication. Such students send their research articles for publication in reputed journals and magazines but language inadequacy becomes a major barrier to their acceptance. Hence it is essential to discuss some viable strategies in order to improve the writing skill of the students. There are various types of writing assignments for the students such as writing different types of letters , writing resume, writing articles, writing essays and writing research papers.

5.1.3 So far as the process of writing is concerned, the teacher should unfold the necessary stages that the students are supposed to undergo. The first stage is concerned with preliminary draft in which the learners are supposed to accommodate as many points as possible. The students may generate ideas by interacting with peers and with resource persons in their concerned fields. The teacher may announce a familiar topic in the class telling the students to develop ideas. The students in this pre-writing would not be possessed by language accuracy least they should interrupt the spontaneous overflow of ideas. However in the second draft grammatical accuracy, use of appropriate words, substitution of sentences and the organization of words and sentences may be undertaken with utmost care. Though the written script which is produced in the class room cannot be incubated but the research articles may certainly be incubated. As a matter of fact if research articles are examined a few days after their completion, the mistakes will easily be detected and hence they may be rectified with ease. In such incubating technique the writer becomes the critical of his own research article. The points to be looked into in a written communication are grammatical and syntactic accuracy, formation of well knitted sentences and logical organization of sentences. In addition, the students should also be taught that the facts of the matter should truly be represented by the choice of words, for example, if one is writing a manual for a machine that has sharp whirling part under a protective cover. This dangerous part could slice off a user's fingers. When one tends to explain how to clean the part one should inform the reader of the danger in manner that prompts him to act cautiously. It will be inappropriate to write "A hazard exists if contact is made with this part while it is whirling". This sentence is not urgent or specific enough to help a user preventing injury. Instead one should write . "warning"Turn of all power before you remove the cover, the blade underneath could slice off your fingers"

In fact, Writing is of varied nature and varied style, hence the students need specific training and practice to master. But in this book I have touched upon only those varieties, which are used in writing different types of letters the students really need to carry on their correspondence. Written communication also includes writing of scientific research articles ,critiques, laboratory reports, manuals, explaining the result of research, describing research procedures and objects and developing paragraphs. In addition to this, technical writers communicate visually with graphs, tables and drawing. To develop competence in any of the aforesaid areas depends mostly on students 'regular practice in the process of writing because the competence in writing will not increase overnight but it requires regular and systematic practice.

5.2.1. Grammar and Writing Skill : By the late 60s the dominant view in both the UK and the USA and possibly through out the English speaking world was that teaching of grammar doesn't improve a child's ability to speak and to write. It was simply a waste of time in the sense that any kind of grammar teaching is better than none. The teaching of traditional and transformational grammar was very boring and hence of little use. But now the attitude has changed. The ELT specialists give importance to the teaching of English but with different strategies and techniques. They are in favour of teaching English grammar through funny and interesting short stories which are based on a particular grammar item. In other words these stories are mini grammar lessons in disguise. Many of the stories contain a lot of dialogues to illustrate how people interact in English. When the learners read the stories they will pick up new phrases that are based on certain grammatical rules. This way the learners enjoy the funny stories and they will absorb the grammar rules automatically without even noticing it. They consider that an essential part of the teaching of any language is the teaching of its grammar. **Weaver**[3] opines Grammar is the term of great antiquity which includes a total mechanism that a language possesses or which determines the rules that the learners use while speaking or writing a language. Hence the knowledge of grammar will enable the learners to use English appropriately and distinguish between well formed and ill formed sentences.

5.2.2. Etymologically the word grammar is related to glamour but it has now become the most unglamorous thing in the world because the formal method of teaching grammar is adopted at every level. The teachers of English regardless of levels apply the same monotonous method of teaching grammar again and again. It has become highly uninspiring and boring. So the method of teaching grammar has to undergo an inevitable reappraisal and new strategies in schools and colleges. Innovative methods have to be evolved for an effective learning of grammar. There is no doubt that the teachers of English must teach the formal knowledge of grammar but the repetition of the same methods and materials must be avoided at the higher level. Communicative grammar must be taught at tertiary level and at the higher level some new methods of teaching of grammar must be evolved. Here I would like to recommend some innovative methods that have emerged from my own practical experience of teaching grammar at higher level.

(I) Generative grammar should be taught to the learners of English at higher level so that they can produce infinite number of sentences. grammatical explanation should be accompanied by numerous illustrations in order to simplify its entire mechanism. This method will improve learner's ability to use English with accuracy and appropriacy.

(II) the teacher can also select passages from the text which can be analyzed to illustrate certain grammatical principles. He has to decide in advance which part of the grammar the learners need to master.The students should be encouraged to detect mistakes between subject and verb agreement in simple sentences. It will be difficult to relate subjects with verbs when they had modifiers in between or when they appear in complex sentences.

Analyzing the paragraph the teacher can state the rules of sentence formation and illustrate how these rules have been observed in the paragraph. In this way what the students have learned formally about grammar at tertiary level will be reinforced and hence they can achieve more grammatical accuracy. The students should be encouraged to detect mismatches between subject and verb agreement in simple sentences. They can identify and relate subjects with verbs

5.2.3. Editing is also an important means for checking grammatical inaccuracy. The students should be given to write a paragraph on the spot. Thus the students should be made aware of the mistakes they have committed in their scripts. Here the teacher should teach prescriptive grammar to the students approving all those sentences which observe the grammatical rules and disapproving those sentences which breach the grammatical rules in some way or the other. In addition to this, the descriptive grammar should also be taught to the students. Here the teacher can state the facts of language as they exist and record sentences as they are spoken or written systematically by a large number of speakers.

The use of computer in teaching and learning grammar is of immense importance. "Computer database can be used by the instructor to classify and differentiate the type of general errors as well as errors committed by learners on account of the influence of the first language". **Williams[4].**Thus it determines the most common errors cross-linguistically and more specifically, the particular form of a particular error type within a particular language group. It will point out subject – verb agreement errors. The base form of verb was over generalised incorrectly more often than the –s form by all speakers. The learners typically omit the articles a/ an more often. A computer can thus analyze the specific mistakes the student has made and can react in a different way from the usual teacher. Thus leads the student not only to self correction , but also to understanding the principles behind the correct solution .

5.3. HOW TO WRITE EFFECTIVE BUSINESS CORRESPONDENCE

Letters are the expression of heart and mind. They are the most important means for giving and seeking information. The success or failure of an organization depends to a large extent on its correspondence. Tactful handling of business correspondence expedites business procedures and open markets. It is well said "A good business letter is a master key that opens locked doors". **Sinha[5]** The writer of a letter is a person communicating with another person. It should be therefore kept in mind that he should be clear, simple, polite and convincing manifesting personal touch in his letter. The modern executive likes to use friendly and conversational style rather than stilted, dull and stiff which was in fashion till about a half century ago. To highlight this point some old fashioned expression used in business correspondence are given below along with suggestions and alternatives.

(a) **Typical Expression:** Enclosed herewith please find cheque to the value of Rs 500

(b) **Reasons for Objection:** (1) Not standard English (11)"Cheque to the value of" seems ridiculous (111) "Herewith" is a pretentious legalism

(c) **Suggested Alternatives :** I enclose a cheque for Rs. 500

(2)

(a) **Typical Expression:** subsequent to your perusal of the documents

(b) **Reasons for Objections:** Verbose and stilted. "perusal" is pompous

(c) **Suggested Alternative :** After you have examined the documents.

(3)

(a) **Typical Expression :** Respectfully yours

(b) **Reasons for Objection:** False complement , unduly servile

(c) **Suggested Alternative :** Yours faithfully

(4)

(a) **Typical Expression :** My overdue account for which a cheque will oblige .

(b) **Reason for Objection :** It is not necessary to state that a cheque will oblige.

(c) **Suggested Alternative :** Will you please send a remittance for The amount outstanding .

(5)

(a) **Typical expression:** At your early convenience

(b) **Reasons for Objection:** Not a normal English idiom, abstract and impersonal.

(c) **Suggested Alternative:** As soon as you can .

(6)

(a) **Typical Expression:** I'm in receipt of your esteemed favour

(b) **Reason for Objection :** verbose, esteemed favour" is obsequious

(c) **Suggested Alternative :** Thank you for your letter.

(7)

(a) **Typical expression :** We shall notify you in due course as to The date of despatch

(b) **Reason for Objection:** verbose, nebulously phrased

(c) **Suggested Alternative:** We shall let you know later when the goods will be sent.

(8)

(a) **Typical expression:** I hope this meets with your requirement and approval.

(b) **Reason for Objection:** It is a stiff style of writing

(C) **Suggested Alternative:** I hope you approve.

(9)

(a) **Typical Expression:** please be advised that you should submit the form before 30th June.

(b) **Reason for Objection:** old fashioned style

(c) **Suggested Alternative:** You should submit the form before 30th June .

(10)

(a) **Typical Expression**: kindly advise/ inform at an early convenient date.

(b) **Reason for Objection**: style is stiff

(c) **Suggested Alternative**; please let me know soon.

5.3.1. Format of Business Letters

Two important formats; (1) British Format (2) American Format are commonly used in business letter writing.

(1) British Format : It is indented form based on the old British conventions. The sample is given below:

Company letter-head
Name and address already printed
Phone, fax no :
E-mail address:

Reference N0: date:

Name and address of addressee

For the attention of salutation

Subject heading often used in business letter

Body of Letter

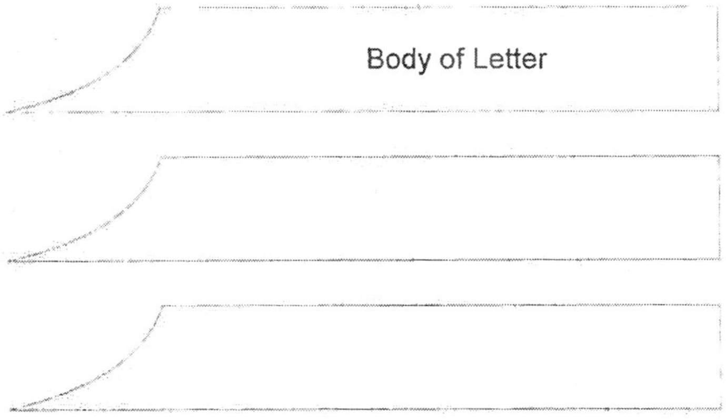

Subscription

Handwritten personal signature

Signatory's typed name
Signatory's position in the company
Company's name

Encl:

Postscript

Ref initials

Note: The greatest advantage of British format is that each paragraph can be easily identified because there is some space left in the beginning.

(2) **American Format:** America format looks more presentable and is easier to handle. It is being followed all over the world. The sample is given below:

Company letter-head

Name and address already printed

(Either in the centre or on the left)

Phone, fax no:

E-mail address

Reference No: Date:

Name and address of Addressee

For the attention of salutation

Subject heading often used in business letter

Body of the letter

Subscription

Signature

Signatory's typed name

Signatory's position in the company

Encl:
Post Script
Ref initials

Example of letters

Associates Construction Corporation

Jamia Urdu Road Aligarh

E-mail No.Mobile No:

Reference No: **May2,2009**

Lucknow Wooden Work
Railway Road
Lucknow

Dear Sir

We are leading Construction contractors and dealers in construction materials in Aligarh. The demand for wooden work is steadily increasing in Aligarh. We have received a large number of enquiries and orders for them.

Please kindly send us your catalogue and price list for wholesale purchase. Since our annual requirements in wooden works of all kinds are large. We would like to place regular orders with you

Hence please quote your most favourable prices and terms. (6)

Yours faithfully

K. K Ansari
Manasger

(1) **"letterhead"** contains the name of the company usually given on the top of the centre.

(1) **Reference No:** Every business letter usually contains a reference number to which the receiver may refer in all the future correspondence.

(2) **Date:** The date is usually written on the right hand side, parallel to the reference number as shown in the letter.

(3) **Addressee:** Name and address of the person to whom the letter is sent.

(4) **Salutation ;** Salutation is the greeting of the addressee which is chosen on the basis of familiarity with the reader. The commonly used salutation is given below.

(I) Dear Sir

(II) Dear Madam

(III) Dear Sir/ Dear Madam

(IV) Dear Mr John

(V) Dear Mrs Jones

(VI) Dear Sirs

(VII) Your Excellency (while addressing the ambassador or High Commissioner of a foreign country.

(VIII) "Gentleman" is used when a circular is sent to many addresses including an individual , firm, society, etc

(5) **Subject Line:** Many offices/ writers use subject line to make the letter more visible

(6) **The Body of the Letter :** It carries the main content generally divided into two or three paragraph

(7) **Subscription or Formal Close**: must match the salutation as shown below :

Dear Sir	Dear Mr. John
Dear Madam	Dear Ms Jones
Sir	Dear Katrina
Yours Faithfully	Yours Sincerely

(8) **Signature Block:** signature of the writer just below the complementary close .

(10) **Enclosures:** Sometimes a letter carries with it some important papers such as copies of certificate, testimonials, cheque etc.

(11) **Postscript:** Postscript is written if the writer has forgotten to mention something important in the letter. In such case the writer is supposed to write the postscript very carefully and precisely.

(12) **CC or Carbon Copy Notation:** Sometimes the same letter is sent to higher authorise or some other persons.

5.3.2. Samples of Business Letters

(1) **Lucknow Wooden Work Fitting Workshop**

Railway Road Lucknow

E-mail No: Phone No:

Reference No: 250 B May 10, 2009

Associate Construction Corporation
Jamia Urdu Road , Akbar market
Aligarh

Dear Sir

Thank you for your enquiry of 2nd May and we are glad to know that you are interested in our products. Our Wooden work fitting is finest and approved by the government. It will give you full satisfaction and get the maximum value of your money.

The enclosed catalogue will give you all the necessary details about the wooden works. In view of the large business promised you will get a special trade discount of 5 percent on all orders and an additional 5 percent on all orders exceeding Rs. 25,000.

We assure you our best services.

Yours faithfully

A.J Gupta
Manager
Lucknow Wooden Work fitting Workshop
Railway Road, Lucknow

Encl: One

(2) Firoz Software Company
New Building, Greater Noida
New Delhi

E-mail No: Mobile No:

Announcement of New Business Opening

Gentlemen:

This is to inform you that The Name of Company is now open and is located at 4500 4th Avenue Greater Noida, New Delhi.

Our store offers a complete and diverse line of computer software packages for both personal and business application. Since we do not represent any individual computer hardware manufacturer, the products that we carry are compatible with many systems.

We are therefore able to offer to our customers a wide range of excellent software packages. Enclosed, for your review, is a partial list of the items we currently have available.

We hope that you will come and visit us soon.

A.C Gupta
4th Avenue, Greater Noida
New Delhi

Enc : 2

(3) Standard Cover Letter in Response to
Inquiry
Ghazi Stores
16, Inner Circle. Connaught Place
New Delhi

The Sales Manager
Unique Boutique Products
16, Andheri, Mimbai

Dear Sir

Thank you for your recent inquiry about (nature of inquiry)

We are enclosing our catalogue and price list for your review and are confident that this detailed literature will provide many of the answers you have requested.

If there is additional information you would like to have regarding our products, please do not hesitate to contact us. We will be most happy to be of assistance.

Thank you for the very kind words you used to describe our line of products.

Yours Sincerely

Ahmad Ghazi
Manager, Ahmad ghazi stores
Cannaught Place
New Delhi

(4) Complementary Letter to Employee on Handling of Emergency

Dear Dr. Rahil

You are to be highly commended for the way that you handled the emergency that occurred yesterday.

The paramedics have informed us that if you hadn't acted as quickly as you did, our customer's attack might have been fatal. Thanks to your fast reaction, she is already out of intensive care and on the road to recovery.

We are very proud of your association with our organization.

Yours Sincerely

Khalid Khan
Firoz Specialist Hospital
Medical Road
Aligarh

(5) Appointment for Employment Interview

Dear Mr.Philip

Thank you for your recent application for employment

with (Name of Company) . An interview has been scheduled for you on Monday,June 7, 2006, at 10:00, with Mr. Phil Menot, Head of Personnel. Mr. Menot's office is located on the 10th floor, Room 1009.

A test will be administered to you immediately following your interview, which will take approximately one hour.

If you are unable to keep this appointment or if you have any questions, please call me at (813) 555-4000.

Yours Sincerely

Dr. Ahmad Bin Waleed
Manager, Glass Manufacturing Company
New Delhi

(6) 30 Day Notice to Quit
NOTICE to quit the rented apartment
Apartment No: 23
Alig Apartment
Shamshad Market
Aligarh

Dear Mr.Shahid

Take notice that your month to month tenancy of the herein described premises is hereby terminated at the expiration of 30 days after service of this notice on you,and that you are hereby required to quit and on said date deliver up to me the possession of the premises now held and occupied by you under such tenancy.

Said premises are known as:

__________(name of building)__________

__________(address)________________

__________(city, state, zip)____________

This is intended as a 30 days' notice to qut, for

the purpose of terminating your tenancy aforesaid.

Dated: ___________________

____

Landlord

(7) Apology for Accounting Errors and Past Due Notices

Dear Dr.Wahid

You deserve an explanation for what went wrong in our accounting department, and I hope that this letter will serve to resolve our recent difficulties.

I know that you can appreciate the fact that it has taken some time to find out exactly what occurred, and, therefore, please accept our apologies for the delay in this response.

Apparently, your payment was received in a timely fashion, but it was credited to an account which bears a similar name to yours. Therefore, we commenced sending you our standard notices requesting payment, in keeping with our routine policy. Even after the posting error was rectified,our accounting department failed to notify our credit department, which is why you continued to receive our correspondence demanding payment.

I know how exasperating this has been for you and I am deeply sorry that it has taken so long to straighten out this problem. While there is a procedure within our firm to preclude this type of error from occurring, we are reinforcing this procedure.

You have been a valued customer of ours for a long time and we appreciate your affording us the opportunity to serve you. You may rest assured that this problem will not surface again.

Yours Sincerely

Name:

Position :

(8) Congratulations on Promotion

Dear Dr. Aiman

Congratulations on your recent promotion to (position)

I know how hard you have worked to earn the recognition you presently enjoy at (name of firm) , and I feel that they are very wise in having made their choice.

Please accept our best wishes for your success in your new position.

Yours Sincerely

Name:

Position and company name

(9) Acknowledgement of Customer praise of Employee

Dear Sir

Thank you for your kind letter regarding your exceptional treatment by one of our employees. A copy of your letter has been forwarded to the personnel department and will be included in the employee's file.

So seldom is it that a customer takes the time to write a letter of appreciation, that I feel moved to reward your initiative.

Please accept the enclosed certificate, which, when presented, will entitle the bearer to a ten percent discount on the merchandise being purchased at that time.

This is but a small token of our appreciation of customers such as you, upon whose satisfaction we have been allowed to grow and prosper in this highly competitive marketplace.

Again, on behalf of our entire organization, a heart-felt

thank you.

Yours faithfully

(10) Application for License

Dear Director

I, (name of applicant), do hereby apply for a license to display the trademark of (association), "(trademark) " at my place of business located at (address) , in the City of , State of .That this application is in accordance with the regulations of the (trade association).

I am cognizant of the regulations of (trade association)that govern the display of said trademark and the manner conducting business, and I agree to abide by such regulations at all times.

Yours Sincerely

Signature

Name and Position

(11) Apology for Delayed Response & Request for Meeting

Gentlemen:

This is to inform you that we are unable to make delivery on the above referenced purchase order on the date indicated.

We should have our merchandise ready to ship within 10 days of the original delivery date and we hope that you can hold off until that time.

We did want to inform you of this delay as soon we were advised in order to give you as much time as possible to make alternate arrangements, if necessary. We can assure you, however, that if your order remains in force we will expedite delivery to you as soon as we have received the merchandise.

Please accept our apology for this delay and thank you for your understanding

Best Regards

Name And Address

(12) Congratulations on outstanding achievements

Dear Mr. Kamil

There is no doubt that your recent achievements will be spoken of for some time to come and that the admiration for your accomplishments is felt by all of us within the industry as well as the general public.

Please accept my heartiest congratulations for your success.

Yours Sincerely

Signature

Name and position

(13) A Shareholder asks about the progress of the company with a view to increasing his shareholding

Dear Sir

A good dividend record in the last six years and a high price in the share market for your company's shares have impressed me very much and I wish to increase my present shareholding in the company. I shall be obliged if you kindly let me know whether the company is contemplating the issue of any Rights Shares or Bonus Shares for the expansion of its activities or whether there is any possibility of increase in the dividend rate this year.

Your advice in the matter will help me greatly.

Yours faithfully

(14) A bank manager informs a customer about a personal loan that the Head Office has agreed to sanction.

Private and Confidential

Dear Sir

Further to our telephonic conversation, I'm glad to inform you that my Head office has agreed to make you a personal loan of up to Rs.250,000. This loan is to be repaid over a period of three years at an interest rate of eighteen percent.

As arranged, we will now be taking a second charge on your property . we have already received the approval of the Building Society to this charge, and we shall be obliged if you would call at this office to complete formalities.

Yours faithfully,

Manager

(15) Letter Informing Non-Selection

Dear Mr/Ms

It was a pleasure meeting you on July 20,2009 at 5.00 p.m in our office. You did very well in the interview. Your C.V. is also very impressive, We wish we could make you an offer that we regret, we find difficult to do at present.

Your application and C.V. are in our file. We assure you that we will get in touch with you as and when we can accommodate you. We are sure a bright and capable person like you will be an asset to any organization. Best wishes.

Sincerely

Job Refusal Letter

Dear Sir/ Madam

It was indeed a pleasure meeting you at Gurgaon. I was deeply impressed by the warmth of the people I met there and the there pleasant atmosphere in the entire office

I was especially impressed to receive the generous offer of appointment sent by you. I would have loved to join your team had I not, in the meanwhile, accepted another job at Faridabad. I thank you again for the kind and courteous treatment shown to me.

Yours faithfully

(16) Employment Cover letter

Writing a cover letter in response to an advertisement

29 Medical Road
Medical Colony
Aligarh
July 25, 2009

The Chief Engineer Indian airways
New Delhi

Dear Sir,

Subject: Application for the Post of a Purchase Officer

With reference to your advertisement in The Times of India dated 22July 2009 for the post of Purchase officer in Indian Airways,I offer my candidature for the said post. As regards my particulars, I attach herewith a copy of my bio-data for your kind consideration.

If given a chance, I assure you Sir, I will carry my duties honestly and earnestly.

Thanking you

Yours faithfully

ABC

5.4. How to Write Curriculum Vitae (C.V.)

It is a kind of bio-data /resume which a person presents while applying for a job. Given below is an example of curriculum Vitae (C.V)

(1) Heading, Name, designation, recent address,E-mailNo and Phone No: in the centre

(2) Career Objective

(3) Outstanding Achievement

(4) Summary of Qualification

(5) Workshops attended so far

(6) Employment History

(7) Over all Work Experience

(8) Research Experience

(9) Relevant Co-Curriculum Activities

(10) Administrative Posts

(11) Computer Knowledge

(12) Hobbies

(13) Publications

(14) Personal Details

(a) Name

(b) Date of Birth

(c) Father's Name

(d) Nationality

(e) Permanent Address(E-mail, Mobile No

(f) Marital status(kids)

(g) Proficiency in Language

(h) Passport No (not essential in National C.V.)

(i) Valid up to

(j) Testimonials and references

(k) Salary expected

(l) **Undertaking:** I the undersigned hereby declare that all the information furnished above are true to my best of faith and belief

(m) Date

(n) Signature

One sample of bio-data is given below

CURRICULUM VITAE

Dr. J. Ahmad (from India)
Asst. Professor of English
Jeddah Community College
King Abdul-Aziz University
E-mail: drjameelahmad@rediffmail.com
Phone No: 00966 -553013719

CAREER OBJECTIVE:

(I) To acquire competence in English language teaching through educational technology at different levels such as ESL (English as a Second Language and EFL (English as a Foreign Language).

(II) To write books on the aforesaid topics on the basis of teaching experience in order to facilitate students' learning process.

Published Books

(1) Structure, Discourse and Teaching of Scientific English

(11) Media Technology and English Language Teaching.

Summary of Qualification

- **Ph.D : in English language Teaching, ELT (applied linguistics)**

  Aligarh Muslim university, Aligarh. India , in 2002.

Topic of Ph.D: Structure and Discourse of Scientific English; A Study of Scientific Research Articles by Non-Native Users of English.

Summary: It strikes difference between scientific use of English and literary use of English. It focuses innovative methods and approaches how to teach scientific English to the students of engineering and medical sciences. It also discuses scientific terminologies and their coinages.

- **M.phil : in English Language Teaching (ELT) A.M.U. Aligarh, India in 1995.**

Topic of M.Phil: Role of Educational Technology in English Language Teaching.

Summary of M.phil : It deals with innovative methods English language teaching through media technology. It focuses the integration of media technology in several methods and approaches for the teaching of English as a second and as a foreign language.

- **M.A. A.M.U. Aligarh. India English Literature, 1992**
- **B. A A.M.U. Aligarh. India English Literature, 1989**

Diploma Courses in CLT: (Communicative Language Teaching)

(1) **PGCTE** (Post Graduate Certificate in English LanguageTeaching) Central Institute of English and Foreign Language, Hyderabad, established in collaboration with British council. India.

(11) **PGDTE** (Post Graduate Diploma in English Language Teaching, CIEFL, Hyderabad. India, established in collaboration with British Council, India.

Note: In fact, my **M.Phil, PhD** degrees and **diploma courses** are related to important issues in the teaching of English as a second language and as a foreign language

Work Shops attended till date

(1) Attended eight workshops and orientation programmes on English Language Teaching (ELT) in India

(II) **Self Study Workshop** (Training prog am conducted by COE ,USA, at JCC, King Abdul Aziz University

(III) **Chairman of Standard Six** (assigned to prepare a draft on Physical Description of Jeddah Community College, Its Health and safety Plan and Maintenance plan.

(IV) Attended a Workshop on Strategic Planning at JCC, Kingdom of Saudi Arabia.

(V) A workshop on the **Development of Excellence and Innovative Teaching.**

Curriculum and Syllabus Designing : I designed a syllabus

(English for Business English) at graduate level A.M.U. Aligarh, India Employment History

(1). **Sub-Editor :** Journal of Islamic Science 1994-95 MAAS, Aligarh. India

(II) **Editor:** MAAS News Letter 1995-96 MAAS Aligarh, India

(III) **Lecturer (English) Dept. of English 1996-2006 A.M.U.Aligarh.India**

(IV) **Teaching of English for Competitive Examinations 2002-2006 Coaching Guidance Centre A. M.U Aligarh, India**

(v) Teaching of Integrated Language Skills from 2006 onwards JCC, Kingdom of Saudi Arabia

Over All Teaching Experience: 13 years teaching experience at different Levels: graduate, post graduate and undergraduate levels.

Teaching Assignment at Different Levels

(1) Teaching of four language skills such as listening, speaking, reading and writing skills through media technology.

(II) Teaching of literature, business English, grammar and phonetics

(III) Teaching of English for specific purposes such as MBA, MFC and Banking Exams.

(IV) Preparing students for group discussions for Civil Services (I.A.S.), MBA, MFC, etc. (India)

(V) Teaching essay writing to the aspirants of Civil Services in India

Research Experience; 8 years in (1) Scientific English (II) Media Technology and English Language Teaching

Relevant Co-curricular Activities;

1. Secretary of Raleigh Literary Society
   1990 Deptt. Of English, AMU.India

2. Secretary of Cultural Society
   1992 Sulaiman Hall, AMU, India

3. Warden Incharge of Lit. & Cult. Society
   1997 RM Hall, AMU, India

4. Supervisor of Literary Magazine
   1997 R.M Hall, A.M.U Aligarh, India

Administrative Post

1. Warden Incharge; A-Block RM Hall, AMU,India, One year

2. School Proctor 10+2, Boys section, AMU, India,Three years

Computer Knowledge; MSWORD, MSEXCEL, MSPOWERPOINT

Hobbies: Writing Articles, writing books and Social interaction.

Publications: articles published in Journals are as follows:

	Title	Name of Journals & Magazines	Year of Publication
1.	Honesty is the Best Policy	Radiance	Feb, 1992
2.	The Act of Suicide is unjustified	Hall Magazine	1994

3.	Politics and Religion	Hall Magazine	1994
4.	Prejudice Against Asian Students	MAAS Newsletter	Jan, 1995
5.	Can a crane eat a crane (Editorial)	MAAS Newsletter	Jan, 1995
6.	Editorial	MAAS Journal of Islamic Science	1994
7.	Environmental and Cultural Pollution	MAAS Newsletter	1995
8.	Oestrogenic Pollutant	MAAS Newsletter	Aug, 1995
9.	An Appraisal of Indian Institution	MAAS Newsletter	Dec, 1995
10.	A view of Scientific English	MAAS Newsletter	April, 1996
11.	Views of contemporary Physicists on Religion and Science	MAAS Newsletter	April, 1996
12.	Decline of Science in Muslim World	MAAS Newsletter	Aug, 1996
13.	A Report on Fourth Proclamation ceremony	MAAS Newsletter	Dec, 1996
14.	A Report on the Third Workshop	MAAS Newsletter	Dec, 1996
15.	Annotated bibliographies	MAAS Journal of Islamic Science	1995 – 1997
16.	Several Interviews	MAAS Newsletter	
17.	Translation of several articles published in Ayah (a reputed Urdu Journal)		
18.	I have been outstanding speaker and creative writer, won several prizes in interhall debate and essay writing competitions in India		
19	**Translated ten scientific articles from English into Urdu**		
20	**Resource person; Material production on the teaching of Business English**		

Pers onal Details

Date of Birth	01.10.1968
Father's Name	Mr. Mohd. Saleem
Nationality	Indian
Address for Correspondence	Jeddah Community College King Abdul Aziz University.Jeddah P.O. Box 80283 Jeddah 215589 Fax: 02 2870024 Kingdom of Saudi Arabia
Permanent Address:	21, Hiba Apartment, Dhorrah Mafi Aligarh, India
Passport No:	E3768918
Marital Status	Married (Four Kids)
Languages Known	English, Urdu, Hindi & Arabic

Dr. J. Ahmad **Date: June3, 2009**

Asst.Professor of English (GRC)

Jeddah Community College, Jeddah

King Abdul Aziz University

Kingdom of Saudi Arabia

P.O.Box 80283 Jeddah 21589

Fax: 02 2870024

5.5. SOME SPELLING RULES

Spelling is one of the major factors to acquire competence in English. Though it is very complicated issue but still there are some simple rules if kept in mind will help learners overcome spelling mistakes. They are as follows:

(1) **With suc(c)-**, ex- and pro-, double e must go. By applying that rule, you can remember how to spell preceding and proceeding and similar words:

Such as: **exceed succeed , proceed**

Concede, precede, recede

(2) **When a word ends with –e** and you add to it , drop the **e** when the addition begins with a vowel or y: such as: Courage/ courageous , bône/ bony , hate/ hating

Note that words ending with – **ce** or –**ge** keep the e when the addition is – able or –ous such as Courage/courageous , notice / noticeable

(3) When a word ends with e and you add to it, keep the **e** when the addition begins with a consonant: Such as

Advance/ advancement, hate/ hateful,

like/ likewise

There are some exception to the rule

Argue/ argument, awe/ awful,

due/ duly, True/ truly

(4) Most words ending with a single consonant double that consonant when addition beginning with a vowel is made. Such as

Blot/ blotting/ blotted , Mat / matting / matted

Begin/ beginning, transmit/ transmitted

Propel/ propelling, refer/ referring,

signal/signalled, travel/ traveller

some Exceptions: develop/ developing/ developed

limit/limiting / limited, profit/ profiting/profited

(6) When –full is joined to another words, it loses one L

Boast / boastful, fear/ fearful

(7) When –**full** is joined to another word ending with double **LL** each word loses one **L**

Full+ fill = fulfil (fulfilled)

Skill + full = skilful (but skilfully)

Will + full = wilful (but wilfull

5.6 PARAGRAPH COMPREHENSION

At the end of the tenth century, a brilliant scientist left his home town of Basra to pursue an ambitious project in Egypt. He had noticed how, seasonally, the river Nile flooded large parts of the delta. But in winter water levels fell so low cultivation was almost impossible. What, he thought, if the surplus flood water could be stored and used when most needed?. He devised a scheme to regulate the Nile, so that the people could derive benefit at its ebb and flow. His plan required building a three way embankment dam near Aswan. He sent the proposal to the Fatimid Caliph al-Hakim in Cairo. The Caliph was impressed ; and issued a royal commission : come to Cairo and build the dam. The young scientist spent several months examining the site , working out the details of how to implement his plans, and it has to be said , spending the generous largesse of the Caliph . But there was a problem : the technology at his disposal was just not up to the task. He came to a sad conclusion : if it were possible to dam the Nile the ancient Egyptians would already have done so. Now , he faced a new problem : how to tell the Caliph ? He devised his most cunning plan –he pretended to be mad. The Caliph retired him to a small office near Al-Azhar university .

The young scientist was Ibnal-Haitham , known to the west as Alhazen . This pretend madman spent the next two decades in his laboratory in Cairo where he developed and refined the technique of experimental method; worked on spherical and parabolic mirrors, spherical aberration, the magnifying power of lenses and atmospheric refraction. He noted how rays of light originate in the object seen and not in the eye – as commonly believed by the Greeks- and correctly explained the apparent increase in size of the and the moon when near the horizon. He formulated the laws of reflection and refraction and proclaimed experiment and empirical investigation the foundation of all scientific work. According to George Sarton, "Ibn Haitham is one of the greatest students of optics of all times". He wrote over 200 books on astronomy, mathematics, physics and philosophy. His greatest achievement, Kitab al Manazir , translated into Latin in the late thirteen century as the Book of Optics , was the first comprehensive treatment of the subject : it influenced Roger Bacon and Kepler and had a major impact on western science.[6]

(Q.N0. 1-5) Read the above paragraphs and answer the questions that are given below:

(1) Why did a brilliant scientist leave his home town?

____

____

(2) What scheme did he devise?

____

____

(3) What proposal did he send to Caliph al – Hakeem in Cairo?

____

____

(4) How many years did al –Haitham spend in his laboratory in Cairo?

____

____

(4) Discuss briefly the scientific achievements he made during his stay in his laboratory in Cairo?

____

____

____

____

(Q.N0.6- 12) Match the following words with their meanings :

(6) ambitious ————	(a) a raised structure
(7) embankment ————	(b) liberal giving (money)
(8) largesse ————	(c) having a desire to achieve a particular goal
(9) parabolic ————	(d) unsoundness or disorder of mind
(10) empirical ————	(e) study of outside earth's atmosphere
(11) astronomy ————	(f) experimental
(12) aberration ————	(g) short fictitious story type

(Q.N0.13- 20) Change the following words into nouns:

Words	Nouns	Words	Nouns
Brilliant	------------------	Implement	--------------------
Experimental	--------------------	Pretend	--------------------
Atmospheric	--------------------	Formulated	--------------------
Comprehensive	--------------------	Proclaim	--------------------

(Q.N0. 21-30) Read the paragraphs carefully and write True or False against them.

Sentences	True	False
(21) Ibn Al-Haitham, a brilliant scientist left his home.	________	________

(22) Ibn al Haitham known to the West as George Sarton. ______ ______

(23) The Caliph of Egypt was impressed by Al-Haitham's proposal. ______ ______

(24) Al-Haitham spent only 8 years in his laboratory in Cairo. ______ ______

(25) Al-Haitham wrote many novels and five act plays in Egypt. ______ ______

(26) Al-Haitham wrote 200 books on astronomy. ______ ______

(27) Kitab al-Manazir was written by George Sarton. ______ ______

(28) The book was translated into English. ______ ______

(29) Kitab al- Manazir influenced roger Bacon and Kepler. ______ ______

(30) In thirteen century the book was considered as the book of Optics. ______ ______

(2) abu Nasr al-Farabi (260- 339 Ah) was born in Farab which is situated in Turkistan near the rivers Jajun and Sayjun. Historians differ on the matters of Farabi's origin because he himself has not left any autobiography. Most of the historians say that Farabi was Turkish in origin. But Ibn Abi Usabiáh opines that he was a Persian because his father was the commander of the army and he belonged to a Persian family.

Al-Farabi, the philosopher is known in the West as Alfarabius Abunazar . He was most outstanding and renowned Muslim scholar of his time. Farabi was the first scholar who established a knowledge and intelligence circle based on a combination of religion and philosophy. Farabi moved to Baghdad in about 900 A.D . Here he perfected his knowledge of Arabic with the well known philologist Ibn Al Sarraj. He got training in medicine by Abu Bashar Matta bin Yunus. In 330 A.H / 942 A.D he accepted invitation from the enlightened Hamadani ruler of Aleppo and joined his court where he continued to live in the company of eminent scholars for the rest of his life.

Farabi was not attracted towards government and administrative posts. Keeping away from the greed of worldly affairs Farabi aimed to achieve the heights of scholarship and intelligence. This is why the courtiers respected him as a wise man. The ruler of Aleppo, Saifullah Hamadani respected him the most. Farabi has written more than 100 books, all in Arabic, that is why he was known as Arab philosopher. He was considered among his contemporaries as having sound knowledge and magnificient theoretical mind, a genius knowing more than 70 languages. He was a mathematician, poet, far sighted benevolent with a bent towards keeping alone.[7]

(Q.N0,1-8) Read the above paragraphs and answer the questions given below:

(1) Where is Farab situated ?

____

____

(2) Which family did Farabi's father belong to?

____

____

(3) Farabi moved to Baghdad in about 900 A.D. What did he learn there?

____

____

(4) What did Farabi aim to achieve in his life?

____

____

(5) How many languages did Farabi know?

____

____

(6) Why did the courtiers of Aleppo respected him most?

____

____

(7) Who gave him training in medicine?

____

____

(8) What was Faeabi's circle of knowledge and intelligence based on?

____

____

(Q.N0. 9-16) Read the paragraphs carefully and tick (") the statements true or false

	Sentences	True	False
(9)	There is a unanimous opinion over Farabi'origin.	______	______
(10)	Farabi wrote a lot about his life and his achievement.	______	______
(11)	His father belonged to an Arab family.	______	______
(12)	Farabi was known in the West Alfarabius.	______	______
(13)	Ibn Al-Sarraj was a philologist.	______	______
(14)	Farabi was very much interested in administrative post.	______	______

(15) Farabi has written more than 100 books. ________ ________

(16) Farabi was known as a Persian philosopher. ________ ________

(Q.N0. 17-26) Write down the adjectives of the following words.

Words	Adjectives	Words	Adjectives
Origin	----------------------	Autography	----------------------
Intelligence	----------------------	Religion	----------------------
Knowledge	----------------------	Arabic	----------------------
Medicine	----------------------	Eminence	----------------------
Administration	----------------------	attraction	----------------------

(Q.N0.27-35) Match the following words with their meanings

Words Meanings

(27) Autobiography ———— (a) standing above others

(28) Outstanding ———— (b) freed from ignorance

(29) Renowned ———— (c) expert in literature and language

(30) Philologist ———— (d) very famous

(31) Contemporary ———— (e) great in deed or exalted

(32) magnificent ———— (f) living during the same period of time

(33) Courtiers ———— (g) biography of a person written by himself

(34) Enlightened ———— (h) attendant in royal court

(35) Eminent ———— (i) standing out from the group

(3) Solar Energy car

Well, we have all heard of a diesel car , an electronic car , even a gas powered car, but car that is run on sunshine is something else again. Nevertheless, a team of engineers from Berkshire have built a solar powered machine that does just what's more what is more they are planning to drive it and right across Europe: all the way from Athens in Greece to Lisbon in Portugal .

The solar powered car is the brainchild of students at university college in Cardiff and it is being developed at intermediate technology at Mortimer near Reading. This is no futuristic gimmick. The car really works doing a healthy 20 miles an hour for a three hour stretch. Solar panels transfer energy to storage batteries which in turn power the electronic motor. Intermediate technologists are confident that car will be successful demonstration of the sun can be tapped usefully and efficiently.

Engineer Bruce Cross has already driven the car from London to Reading. How realistic a project is it to think that you can cross Europe using no other power at all? He has demonstrated that solar energy can be used usefully to produce power in a reasonable quantity. He is trying to demonstrate that a solar car is a very useful way of getting around, but it can be used for many other purposes, like refrigeration for ...... storage like water pumping and protection of pipe line. There is some wild driving on the continent and he is doing miles a hour a foot of the ground. He will have a poped running along twenty yards behind him and he hopes that will give normal visibility to him. The engineer will set out from Athens on June 21st by which time he hopes to have raised another 2.00 in sponsorship. The boffins from Mortimer are put to prove that the sun can be harnessed to provide help for nations whose problems can't be solved by money alone.[8]

(Q.N0. 1-5) Match the words with their meanings.

	Words		Meanings
(1)	Trial ————	(a)	boards for instruments
(2)	demonstrate ————	(b)	to produce power
(3)	panels ————	(c)	testing and trying
(4)	to harness ————	(d)	to be seen
(5)	visibility ————	(e)	show clearly by proof

(Q.N0 6-10) Give the meanings of the following words.

(6) Brain child ____________________

(7) Storage batteries ____________________

(8) Boffins ____________________

(9) Tapped ____________________

(10) Sponsorship ____________________

(Q.N0. 11-15) Explain the following phrases :

(11) Borne out ____________________

(12) Small scale application ____________________

(13) Put out ____________________

(14) Futuristic gimmick ____________________

(15) Wild driving ____________________

(Q.N0.16-20) Answer the following questions .

(16) What were the ambitious plan of the engineers for driving the solar energy car ?

____

____

____

____

(17) What are the advantages of a solar energy car ?

____

____

____

____

(18) Can you see solar energy for other purposes?

____

____

____

____

(19) What were the technologists sure about their inventions ?

____

____

____

____

(20) If you are driving a solar energy car how will you save it from accident ?

____

____

____

____

(Q.N0.21- 25) Change the following words into adjectives.

Words	Adjectives
Produce	----------------------------------
Protection	----------------------------------
Calculation	----------------------------------
Efficiently	----------------------------------
Machine	----------------------------------

(4) The holistic benefits of yoga are too well known to detail here. Besides the current celebrity endorsements and mushrooming of yoga schools worldwide, the teaching and practice of different kinds of yoga is a hallowed and popular tradition in India. However teaching and learning of yoga should not become counterproductive. That is why the plan proposed by the National Council for Educational research and Training (NCERT) to introduce compulsory yoga in schools from class V1 onwards in all states may not be in the best interests of the students.

The teaching and learning of yoga cannot be straitjacketed to suit constraints of time, space and faculty of availability. It is a discipline which demands that the taught are given individual attention. A few yogic postures might appear simple but they demand a great deal of practice and discipline from the student and precise teaching from the master, who is expected to tailor the intensity and duration of the session to suit the individual's flexibility , willingness and threshold levels. Failing to pay close attention to these details could lead to situations which harm the child rather than benefit his health.

Yoga is difficult discipline whose techniques are learnt slowly over a period of time. To create more demand for it than there qualified teachers would dilute the quality of instruction as well as encourage fly-by-night self-taught yoga masters to compete for teaching posts to ensure regular income and job security for themselves. Considering that schools are hard put to find qualified and effective teachers of subjects.[9]

(Q.N0.1-6) Read the above paragraphs carefully and answer the questions given below:

(1) What plan did The National Council for Educational research and Training Propose to introduce?

____

____

____

____

(2) Does yoga require a regular practice or is it easier to do without practice?

(3) " Failing to pay close attention to these details could lead to situations which harm the child rather than benefit his health". Explain

(4) " The teaching and learning of yoga cannot be straitjacketed to suit constraints of time, space and faculty of availability". Explain

(5) "However teaching and learning of yoga should not become counterproductive" explain

(6) Would it be difficult to find qualified teachers for yoga?

(Q.No.7-15) Read the paragraphs and tick (") the statements true or false.

Sentences		True	False
(7)	Yoga is a new tradition in India.	———	———
(8)	NCERT is in favor of introducing yoga in school.	———	———
(9)	teaching and learning of yoga should be counterproductive.	———	———
(10)	Yoga requires no practice at all.	———	———
(11)	Its careless teaching can harm the students a great deal.	———	———
(12)	It is difficult to find qualified teachers for yoga.	———	———
(13)	Yoga is a discipline to be learnt slowly over a period of time.	———	———
(14)	Introducing yoga in the schools is not in the interest of the students.	———	———
(15)	Yoga should not made compulsory in the schools.	———	———

(Q.N0. 16 -22) Match the following words with their meanings.

(16) Holistic ——— (a) to adapt to new

(17) Celebrity ——— (b) a piece of timber that lies under a door

(18) Mushroom ———(c) to make thinner or liquid

(19) Straitjacket ———(d) complete

(20) Dilute ———— (e) an enlarged complex

(21) Threshold ———— (f) restrict

(22) Flexibility ———— (g) a famous person

(Q.N0. 23-30) Change the following words into nouns .

Words	Nouns
Holistic	------------------------
Counterproductive	------------------------
Available	------------------------
Individual	------------------------
Qualify	------------------------
Dilute	------------------------
Ensure	------------------------
Encourage	------------------------

(5) The solution to any problem begins with a diagnosis. My optimism is based on the fact that diagnosis has already begun. Increasingly, the realization is growing that science is important not just for the prosperity of Muslim societies, not just for the purpose of economic development, or for misplaced political vanity or notions of defense based on acquiring nuclear weapons but that science matters because it is vital for the recovery and survival of Islam itself. Just as the spirit of Islam in history was defined by its scientific enterprise, so the future of Muslim societies will depend on their relationship to science and learning. This is the main message of the Arab Human Development Report of 2003. this ground breaking report on "building a Knowledge Society" frankly admits Muslims cannot merely continue to blame everything on colonialism and the West. Muslim states have failed, by their own Islamic standards, the challenge of independence. The report blames authoritarian thought, lack of autonomy in

universities, the sorry state of libraries and laboratories, and under-funding in the Arab world.

Moreover the report recognizes the conceptual problems of interpretation and declares "time has come to proclaim those positive religious texts that cope with current realities". In particular it calls for reviving "ijtihad"as the driving force for change. Indeed, it is now widely argued science can play an important role not just in re-establishing "ijtihad" but in making Islam whole again, reuniting reason once again with revelation. Thus, the revival of science and a reform agenda for Islam in Muslim society need to proceed hand in hand.

No one should be in any doubt –Muslims have a deep emotional attachment to their scientific heritage. But contemporary Muslim society needs more than nostalgic pride in a long departed Golden Age. Instead of cherishing the ashes of burnt out fire -- they need to transmit its flame. Rekindling the flame must mean more than simply eulogizing a list of achievements. It has to focus on instilling the way of thinking, the critical consciousness and methodologies that made Islamic science possible; and it must make this way of thinking and knowing relevant to contemporary times.[10]

(Q.N0.1-10) Read the above paragraphs carefully and answer the questions given below:

(1) What, according to the writer, the solution of any problem ?

____

____

(2) " Increasingly, the realization is growing" . What realization is the writer talking about? .

____

____

(3) What does the future of Muslim depend on?

____

____

(4) What is the Arab Development Report about ?

____

____

(5) " it calls for reviving" ijtihad" as the driving force for change" Explain

____

____

(6) " The revival science and a reform agenda for Islam in Muslim Societies need to proceed hand in hand" Explain.

____

____

(7) What does the contemporary Muslim society really need to do?

____

____

(8) "Rekindling the flame must mean more than simply eulogizing a list of achievements" Explain

____

____

(Q.N0. 9- 15) Match the following words with their meanings.

	Words		Meanings
(9)	Optimism ________	(a)	show affection
(10)	prosperity ________	(b)	state of being self governing
(11)	vanity ________	(c)	the condition of being successful

(12)	autonomy ————	(d)	inflated pride
(13)	cope with ————	(e)	hope
(14)	heritage ————	(f)	praise
(15)	Cherish ————	(g)	to match with the given time
(16)	Eulogize ————	(h)	to put in
(17)	Instill ————	(i)	to revitalize
(18)	Rekindling ————	(j)	property that descends to an heir

(Q.N0.19 25) Write True or False against each statement.

	Sentences	True	False
(19)	Science is vital for revival of Islam.	———	———
(20)	The future of Muslim doesn't depend on science	———	———
(21)	The author wants to criticize west and colonialism	———	———
(22)	Muslim societies just need nostalgic pride.	———	———
(23)	Muslim societies need to instill new thinking.	———	———
(24)	Muslims have emotional attachment to Islamic heritage	———	———
(25)	Science can play an important role in reestablishing ijtihad.	———	———

(Q.N0. 26-32) Write adjectives of the following words.

Words	Adjectives
Problem	---------------------------
Optimism	-----------------------------
Prosperity	--------------------------------
Independence	---------------------------------
Nostalgia	--------------------------------
Methodology	--------------------------------
Possibility	Possible

REFERENCES

(1) Carroll,J. (1958) Psycholinguistics and The Teaching of English Composition. Oxford University Press. London.

(2) Corbett,G. (1985) Media technology and Writing Skill. Cambridge University Press. London.

(3) Weave, Constance .(1996) Teaching Grammar in Context. Postmouth, NH Heinemann.

(4) Williams, Geoff. (1995) Learning Functional Grammar Through Grammar.Oxford University Press. London

(5) Sinha, K.K.(200) Business Communication. Gagotia Publishing Company. New Delhi.

(6) Sardar,Ziauddin,.(2006) Islam and Science Beyond the Troubled Relationship. Journal of Islamic Science, Vol 22 , p.64

(7) Al-Farabi , (2006) A Link between Greek and Islamic Thought. Journal of Islamic Science. Vol.22. p.107

(8) Antony, K. (1995) Solar Energy Car, Future, 5 (15) 30.

(9) Yoga in School Curriculum, The Times of India, 2009.

(10) Maroof Shah, M. (2009) modern science and Varieties of Muslim .Modernism, Islamic Science 4(12)3.

CHAPTER-VI

CONCLUSION

6.1 With a view to promoting learner's proficiency in language skills, the use of educational technology in present pedagogical scenario seems to be almost indispensable. By virtue of its visual presentation, educational technology is capable of arousing maximum motivation which is one of the most essential factors for effective learning. Motivation is, in fact, the crucial force that yields the best result in every kind of learning, particularly in English language learning. Due to lack of motivation, any method or technique used in language pedagogy will certainly fail to promote competence in language skills. Motivation is of paramount importance not for the learner only but the teacher should also be equally motivated so that he can enthusiastically act as a consummate motivator.

The most important question that often emerges in any ELT seminar is as to how to increase learners' motivation. In view of this query, it is often suggested that the teacher should be innovative. Thus the whole discussion comes to an end leaving the learners with no reasonable panacea, but there is no reason that the language experts can't find and prescribe solution for learners' lack of motivation. As regards the motivation, it seems indispensable to describe that the most obvious classroom procedure for promoting learners' motivation is the frequent use of the media technology, because it opens up a rich stimulus for both the learner and the teacher and thus makes them more receptive to the visual presentation. Visual presentation propels the learners to get involved actively in the learning process of English language.

Along with the technological progress, the attitude towards language teaching and learning in developed countries has undergone drastic change. The learners have become more technical minded, so they feel utmost pleasure in using educational technology in the classroom. On account of its having immense motivating force, educational technology has made large strides in the field of education and language teaching in developed countries, but in India and other developing countries, the people are possessed with the notion that educational technology will decentralize teachers and minimize their importance. Keeping this in view, it has been attempted in the very beginning of this study to dispel such fear which is very common among the teachers. The fact is that teacher always remains central in the classroom for his ability to manipulate interesting exercises and interactive communication.

6.2 The main thrust of this book is on the integration of media technology into traditional methods of teaching used for the teaching of language skills. How can the conventional methods, particularly Direct Method and Audio Lingual Method be supported by media technology has also been touched upon in this study. It aims at providing rationale that how media can act as powerful tools in the hands of the teachers to achieve the objects advocated by the text or a method it embodies. The main function of Direct and Audio Lingual Methods is to persuade learners to repeat dialogues and drills read out by the teacher. This can be performed well by tape recorder and video recorder, because they can be stopped and rewound again and again. Besides this, the standard materials which have already been prepared by BBC are easily available. These standard materials contain proper accent, intonation and native speech patterns . If learners listen to them carefully, their language skills will improve enormously. They can speak with proper accent and intonation of the target language. The native model of accentuation patterns will boost up their confidence level and hence facilitate to achieve native like communication.

So far as the communicative method is concerned educational technology prepares the learners for better communication activity. Social interaction activities are seen many times on television and video screen which place much emphasis on social as well as functional aspects of communication and hence acquaint learners with wider variety of communicative situation. Viewing television also wards off the complexity and vagueness.

Visual presentation which the television and video provide enables learners to infer the meaning of language being used in particular context. The use of radio, television, and video will probably lead us to a greater awareness of the concerned subject and thus facilitate learners' understanding of theoretical features of language. A lot of necessary information along with rich vocabulary, the learner gathers from radio, television and video will certainly muster enough confidence in learners and minimize their hesitation.

6.3 The shift of emphasis in the new curriculum to the new approach is from teaching to learning, with the focus on equipping the learner with essential language skills and granting him confidence to use the language effectively in real life situation. The competence in four language skills namely listening, speaking, reading and writing can be doubly enhanced by educational technology. This study attempts to analyze in some details as to how language skills can be facilitated by use of media technology. In the last ten years listening comprehension has begun to be taken seriously. Previously, where there was no interest at all, it seemed to be assumed that the student will just pick it up somehow in the general process of learning of the foreign language. It seems reasonable to assume that the learners would learn to understand it if dialogues are heard repeatedly. They would of course understand the language dialogue gradually if oral drills are well conducted by tape and video, because any dialogue or speech can be heard and reheard by stopping and rewinding them again and again. Moreover, intensive exposure to the standard model presented by audio-video cassettes lays cumulative effect on speaking skills because it acquaints the learner with variety of communication arising from the events of every day life.

One of the major goals of language pedagogy is to teach writing which is often perceived as an awesome task. How to teach writing in the classroom has been one of the most difficult problems for the teacher. The teacher will have to deduce effective devices in order to make the learner effective writer, but due to gross negligence students have suffered a lot in writing. There is no doubt that writing process is extremely exhausting but it can be made exciting by the use of technology. The concluding chapters evaluate how writing can be made more motivating by internet facilities.

Experience has proved that computer does enrich language vocabulary by providing the learner a number of substitute words which do facilitate writing process. Television and computer are considered to be more feasible for writing because they present environment for discovering, creating and shaping ideas. Visual presentation sparks off the writer's imagination and provokes his thought. Apart from that various interviews, dialogues, good conversation and intensive information gathered from television, video and internet promote learner's awareness and develop clarity which is a stepping stone for effective writing. Visual presentation also stimulates sense perception which puts learner's contemplation at work and thus develops creative expression. Here the major focus is on writing of business letters. So many samples of business letters are available on internet . They can immensely benefit the learners of English who want to achieve competence in the writing of business letters. Numerous samples of business letters representing different situations have been taken from internet and incorporated in the book so that the learners can read thoroughly and learn how to write business letters effectively. In brief there is no harm in making an emphatic assertion that educational technology promotes immense motivation in language pedagogy and trains the learners adequately in language skills. There is no doubt that statistical survey has not been undertaken during the course of this study but it has been strongly supported by the interviews taken from highly efficient people. Their opinions and arguments were very encouraging in favor of the media technology for English language teaching. Keeping various arguments and suggestions which have gone in favor of media technology it can be summed up that the introduction of media technology in language class will bring about substantial change in our attitudes to language teaching. It will also bring spectacular progress in learning language skills because of its compelling motivation. Moreover the growing popularity of media technology indicates that the time is not far of when our ordinary classroom will be changed into electronic room for English language teaching.

Bibliography

Acquisition. Cambridge University Press. P.55

Al-Farabi , (2006) A Link between Greek and Islamic Thought. Journal of Islamic Science. Vol.22. p.107

Balaaco, Simon. (1998) Comprehension, the Key to Second Language

Bickel, B and Truscello, D. (1996) TESOL Technology : New Opportunities for Learning : Styles and Strategies with Computers . TESOL Journal , pp. 15-19

Butler- Pascoe, Mary Ellen, (1995). A National Survey of the Integration of Technology into TESOL Master's Programs. Technology and Teacher Education Annual. pp.98-101

Carroll,J. (1958) Psycholinguistics and The Teaching of English Composition. Oxford University Press. London.

Christophersen, P. (1956) An English Phonetic Course. London, Longmans.

Cole, R. (1931) Modern Foreign Language and Their Teaching . New York P.58

Collins Cobuild English Language dictionary

Corbett,G. (1985) Media technology and Writing Skill. Cambridge University Press. London.

Geddes and Sturtridge. (1982) Ed. Video in the Language Classroom in the Use of Video Films.by David Kerridge London P, 113

Gimson.A.C. (1967) English Pronunciation Practice. London, University of London Press.

Hancock, Allan. (1997) Planning for Educational Mass Media , London 5

Hunt, N., & Disdier ,A (1994) Teaching future teachers to enhance teaching and learning with technology. Technology and Teacher Education Annual. (1993) (pp. 178-182)

Jack, Lonergan: (1984) Video in Language Learning, London, P. 1

Krashen, Stephen. (1989). Language Acquisition and Language Education. New York: Prentice Hall International.

Lonergan ,J. (1984) Video in Language Teaching. p 25

Lonergan, J. (1983) Video Application in English Language in ELT documents Oxford, P. 74

Lonergan,J. (1983) Video in Language Teaching, London , P.24

Mac Lean , R.(1968) Television in Education , London. PP. 11-12

Maroof Shah, M. modern science and Varieties of Muslim Modernism Bibliography New Delhi.

Newmark,L. (1971) A Minimal Language Teaching Program, Cambridge University Press. P.25

Norman Lewis (1994) Word Power Made Easy. General Book Depot, Naisarak , Delhi.

OP.Cit : p 18

Rivers, Wilga , M. (1968) Teaching Foreign Language Skills, London, Oxford University Press. P.18

Sardar,Ziauddin,.(2006) Islam and Science Beyond the Troubled Relationship. Journal of Islamic Science, Vol 22 , p.64

Sethi,J. (2008) A Practical Course in English Pronunciation, PHI Learning Private Limited.

Sherrington, Richard, (1973) Television and Language Skills, London, P. 12

Sinha, K.K.(200) Business Communication. Gagotia Publishing Company.

Sinha,K.K . (2002) Business Communication, Galgotia Publishing Company, Karol Bagh, New Delhi.

solar energy Car

Weave, Constance .(1996) Teaching Grammar in Context. Postmouth, NH Heinemann.

Widdowson, H. G. (1979) Teaching Language as Communication. Oxford University Press. P. 58

Williams, Geoff. (1995) Learning Functional Grammar Through Grammar Oxford University Press. London

Wills , J (1983) "The Role of Visual Element in Spoken Discourse " in Video Application in Language teaching , ELT Document 114 England. P. 30

Wills, Jane. (1995) The Role of The Visual Element in Spoken Discourse in Video Application in English Language Teaching. Ed, Brumfit, C,J. Oxford.

Winitz, H. (1975) Comprehension and Problem Solving Strategies for Language Training . Oxford University Press. London. p.89

Yoga in School Curriculum, The Times of India

BIBLIOGRAPHY OF JOURNALS

(1) Applied Linguistics

(2) Audio Visual Language Journal

(3) Behavior

(4) British Journal of Psychology

(5) British Journal of Language teaching

(6) BBC London Calling

(7) British Journal of Educational Technology

(8) ELT Journal

(9) Educational Review

(10) Educational Broadcasting International

(11) Educational Media international

(12) Foreign Language Annals

(13) IRAL

(14) Journal of Applied Behavior Analysis

(15) TV Studies

(16) Journal of Educational Television and Other Media

(17) Journal of Applied Educational Studies

(18) Journal of Speech and Hearing Disorder

(19) Journal of Verbal Learning and Verbal Behavior

(20) Modern Language Journal

(21) Modern English Teacher

(22) Modern English International

(23) World Language English

BIBLIOGRAPHY OF VIDEO MATERIALS

(1) Bid for Power : BBC English by Radio and Television. 1982. An Intermediate Course in Business English for adults.

(2) Challenges : BBC English by Radio and Television (1978) supplementary Course Material in English at advanced Level for Children and Adults.

(3) Canedy Time : BBC English by Radio and Television (1982) Supplementary Materials in English at an Elementary Level.

(4) ESP Business : Nelson Filmscan , (1982) An Advanced Course in Engineering English for Adults.

(5) The Bellerest Story: BBC English by Radio and Television, (1973) An Advanced Course

(6) Television English : BBC English by Television and the British Council (1985)

(7) Telemagazine April : Brighton Language Centre.

(8) Telemagazine May : Brighton Language Centre .

(9) Video Film : Sound of Music

(10) Video Film : Passage to India

(11) Vistron : The Language of Presentation. Longman

(12) Video English : Macmillan,(1983)

◆ ◆ ◆